The INDIA I Saw

S. Ambujammal (1899–1981) was born into great wealth, her father being a top-ranking lawyer of Madras, yet she chose a life typical of many women of colonial India, who at huge personal sacrifice opted to serve the nation. She underwent imprisonment for the cause and later, post India's Independence, dedicated her life to social service. On the passing of the Mahatma in 1948, she founded the Srinivasa Gandhi Nilayam, named after her biological and spiritual fathers (Sriman Srinivasa Iyengar and M.K. Gandhi), an organization devoted to women's welfare which continues to operate even today. She was awarded the Padma Shri by the Government of India.

A memory keeper by passion, **Sriram V.** delves deep into the history of India, particularly South India and the city of Chennai. He has authored over 25 books on subjects including Carnatic music, corporate biographies, and Chennai. Sriram writes for *The Hindu* and is editor of *Madras Musings*, the fortnightly dedicated to Chennai's built, natural and cultural heritage. He is also Secretary of the Music Academy, Madras, in which capacity he is the convenor of its annual conference in December.

The
INDIA
I Saw

An Autobiography

S. AMBUJAMMAL

Translated from the Tamil original by
Sriram V.

Published by
Rupa Publications India Pvt. Ltd 2024
7/16, Ansari Road, Daryaganj
New Delhi 110002

Sales centres:
Bengaluru Chennai
Hyderabad Jaipur Kathmandu
Kolkata Mumbai Prayagraj

Copyright © Srinivasa Gandhi Nilayam 2024
Translation copyright © Sriram V. 2024

The views and opinions expressed in this book are the author's own and
the facts are as reported by her to the best of her knowledge/memory
and which have been verified to the extent possible,
without any intention to cause harm, injury or damage.
The publishers are not in any way liable for the same.
The contents of this book reflect the views of the author and the
translator. The Tamil Nadu Textbook and Educational Services
Corporation is not responsible for the same.

All rights reserved.
No part of this publication may be reproduced, transmitted,
or stored in a retrieval system, in any form or by any means,
electronic, mechanical, photocopying, recording or otherwise,
without the prior permission of the publisher.

P-ISBN: 978-93-5702-738-0
E-ISBN: 978-93-5702-664-2

First impression 2024

10 9 8 7 6 5 4 3 2 1

Printed in India

This book is sold subject to the condition that it shall not, by way
of trade or otherwise, be lent, resold, hired out, or otherwise circulated,
without the publisher's prior consent, in any form of binding or
cover other than that in which it is published.

MISSION STATEMENT

This is an initiative of the Tamil Nadu Textbook and Educational Services Corporation (TNTB & ESC) under the aegis of one of the announcements for the year 2021–22, titled "Thisaidhorum Dravidam" by Honourable Minister for School Education Thiru. Anbil Mahesh Poyyamozhi to identify and translate into English, Kannada, Malayalam and Telugu, Tamil literary works, that they might enhance the reach of Tamil antiquity, tradition and contemporaneity and enrich World literature and to also translate significant literary voices from other Dravidian languages into Tamil. Both ventures are to be undertaken as either independent or joint publications with collaborating publishers.

Members, Academic Advisory Committee (Translation)
1. Dr. R. Balakrishnan, IAS, Researcher and Writer
2. Thiru. S. Ramakrishnan, Writer
3. Thiru. S. Madasamy, Educationist

Project Execution Team
1. Thiru. Dindigul I. Leoni, Chairperson, TNTB & ESC
2. Dr. P. Sankar, IAS, Managing Director, TNTB & ESC
3. Dr. M. Kuppusamy, Member Secretary, TNTB & ESC
4. Dr. T. S. Saravanan, Joint Director (Translations), TNTB & ESC
5. Dr. P. Saravanan, Assistant Director (Publications), TNTB & ESC
6. Thiru. M. Appanasamy, Consultant, TNTB & ESC
7. Tmt. Mini Krishnan, Co-ordinating Editor, TNTB & ESC

The publisher has no objection to this English translation being used to facilitate transfers into other languages.

Contents

Translator's Note: Portrait of a Patriot — ix

1. Sriman Seshadri Iyengar — 1
2. The Vembakkam Clan — 9
3. My Childhood Memories — 23
4. Madurai Grandfather — 34
5. Vande Mataram — 47
6. Gandhiji's Failure — 172

Translator's Note
Portrait of a Patriot

I first came across the name of S. Ambujammal almost 25 years ago when the late Randor Guy, one of Chennai's most popular writers of social history, gave a talk on the lawyers of Madras. During that talk, he dwelt at length on Sriman Srinivasa Iyengar, Ambujammal's father, on his enormous residence Amjad Bagh, and on the various conflicts within that aristocratic household. To me, it all seemed the stuff of drama—a domineering father, a retiring mother, a daughter with a failed marriage wanting to do something, and a son who had had his share of tragedies and dreamt of a career in business, which his father would not allow. And along came Mahatma Gandhi who, like a leading light, showed everyone the way.

Years later, I managed to lay my hands on Ambujammal's autobiography, *Naan Kanda Bharatam*. In that pre-digital era, this was a photocopy of the original, and I read it many times over. Ambujammal had me enthralled. Born into wealth, she could have led a privileged life, only attending governors' garden parties, hobnobbing with the high and mighty of Madras society, spending her summers at hill stations like Ootacamund and Kodaikanal. That she chose to be different is what makes her stand out. Rejecting all material pleasures as ephemeral, she voluntarily took to a difficult path—one of simplicity and sacrifice. This required a retiring personality to transform and seek a role in public life. By doing so, she went against the wishes of the establishment and her parents, in particular her father whose word to her was law. She followed a higher calling, in which she found self-actualization.

Ambujammal's autobiography may not qualify as high literature. Its tone is simple, even artless. But this is what makes it stand out. In true Gandhian style, Ambujammal reveals her life with total honesty. There are no judgements made; she leaves it all to the reader. It also depicts an era gone by, one that is sometimes too fantastic to even seem real. Arranged marriages with grooms never seen before, unheard-of pieces of jewellery, unbelievable orthodoxy, golden cages in which women of the upper class lived, the drama of the freedom struggle, two world wars, the saintly presence of Mahatma Gandhi, pilgrimages to various places lasting months on end—in short, a way of life that seems to be lost forever.

I would like to thank Smt. Mini Krishnan for getting me to translate this autobiography. It was a pleasure working with her—being almost a continuous series of rallies in tennis terms. She was that quick in her editing and returning the chapters to me.

My gratitude is due in no small measure to Smt. Sudha Srinivasan and Smt. Lalitha Ramanujam of the Srinivasa Gandhi Nilayam for readily agreeing to my translating the

Translator's Note: Portrait of a Patriot xi

work, and also for helping me with archival photographs.

Thanks to Karthik Bhatt, my research associate, William Satish for the archival photographs from Srinivasa Gandhi Nilayam, and Malvika Mehra for digitally cleaning these up.

Finally, I am thankful to Dibakar Ghosh and his team at Rupa Publications for agreeing to publish *The India I Saw: An Autobiography*, the English translation of *Naan Kanda Bharatam*—Ambujammal's autobiography in Tamil.

I dedicate this book to Mahatma Gandhi, without whom the Ambujammal we commemorate would have never evolved.

Sriram V.
Chennai, 2024

1

Sriman Seshadri Iyengar

Kanyakumari, located at the southern tip of India, has been considered a sacred spot since time immemorial. It got its name from the penance Goddess Parvati—the daughter of the Himalayas—performed here while she was a virgin[1]. But above all, this is a place endowed with something both natural and unique! Sunrise is always a wonder—it is impossible for anyone to take in all the colours that appear at that time. It is only in Kanyakumari that, having feasted your eyes on the sunrise, you can return to the same spot at the end of the day and thrill to the sun gradually dipping into the western horizon. You can gaze at this forever. When there is such natural glory in Kanyakumari, does the place need any man-made embellishment?

Several sacred spots associated with the Ramayana

---

[1]'Kanya' and 'kumari', both words in Sanskrit, mean 'virgin'.

such as Adi Setu[2], Thiruppullani[3] and Dhanushkoti[4] are close to Kanyakumari. In those days, these regions were ruled by the Setupati Rajas of Ramanathapuram[5]. The present-day eponymous district comprises Sivaganga, Ramanathapuram, Thiruppullani, Devakottai, Karaikkudi, Rameswaram, Utharakosamangai, Paramakudi, the port of Thondi, Muthukulathur, Kadaladi and Manamadurai[6]. The native population comprises those belonging to the Kallar, Maravar and Agampadiyar communities, collectively known as the Mukkulattor[7]. They are all people of powerful physique, rather forbidding in appearance. The women are no exception.

---

[2] Known as Adam's Bridge and now referred to as Ramar Setu, this rock formation is considered synonymous with the bridge the army of monkeys built to help Rama cross over to Lanka.

[3] Literally 'bed of grass'; Rama is said to have reclined here on grass to meditate on the Lord of the Oceans to obtain permission to cross over to Lanka. Even today, a massive idol of a reclining Rama is worshipped in the temple here.

[4] The southernmost tip of India, it is said to have been formed by Rama placing his bow here; Dhanushkoti literally means 'tip of the bow'.

[5] Known as the principality of Ramnad during British times, it was an administrative unit under the Madurai Nayaks in the seventeenth century, governed by territorial heads who later declared themselves independent. The kingdom became a zamindari or fiefdom under the British. The rulers bore the title of Setupati (Protector of the Bridge) as the Rameswaram Temple (also known as Setu due to the bridge built to help Rama cross over to Lanka) came under their jurisdiction.

[6] The districts have since been divided again.

[7] Literally 'those of three communities' (*mu*—3; *kulam*—community).

The Zamindar of Sivaganga[8] needed someone to oversee his estate and be a guardian to his minor son. In those days, there was no prerequisite qualification for such appointments—native intelligence was all that was needed. The Zamindar, on coming to know Sriman Seshadri Iyengar of Sivaganga possessed this very attribute, appointed him as the overseer of his estate.

Madurai and its adjoining Ramanathapuram districts have been known for the encouragement they gave to the growth of Tamil. Scholarship in that language is greatly valued in these regions. Seshadri Iyengar was adept in Tamil; he was also a Sanskrit scholar. Owing to his skilful handling of all assignments, he rose rapidly in the service of the Sivaganga Estate and soon became its Agent—one of the highest positions possible.

Those were times when you did not need a degree in law to argue your cases in courts. Nor did law colleges exist. Anybody who had the skill to express his client's arguments clearly and well, and explain in Tamil the nuances of Hindu Law and the Code of Manu, could pay the necessary fee and get the *sanad*[9] to practice as a *vakil*[10]. Large estates were forever embroiled in litigation. Why, there were zamindars who had fought cases all the

---

[8] A zamindari like Ramnad, with a similar history. Both remain districts of present-day Tamil Nadu.
[9] A charter or diploma.
[10] In pre-independent India, there was a clear distinction between barristers, invariably qualified in England, and vakils, who specialized in Indian law.

way up to the Privy Council in London over matters as trivial as two palm trees! They were not concerned about profit or loss. Ownership and prestige were all that mattered to them, and they considered it their duty to establish these at all costs. In such matters, Seshadri Iyengar soon acquired the reputation of being invincible.

The stories of his victories in court soon reached the ears of the Setupati of Ramanathapuram. The then ruler was embroiled in a very difficult court case. He had been adopted as heir to the kingdom, and this had been legally challenged. The progress of the case was not satisfactory. He, therefore, sought the help of the Sivaganga Zamindar and requested that Seshadri Iyengar be sent over to assist him. As a consequence, Seshadri Iyengar shifted to Ramanathapuram. He was given a palatial residence on the southern bank of the Big Tank. It was to serve as his office as well. The household comprised other than him, his wife and a widowed sister. He had no children.

The kingdom included several villages where some or the other problem would crop up. It was Seshadri Iyengar who would be sent to enquire, pass judgement, and re-establish peace. He, therefore, had to travel often. While returning from one such tour, he brought back a beautiful woman. Pausing at the doorstep, he asked his wife to perform the traditional *aarati*[11] as would be done for a newlywed couple. The wife immediately realized what had transpired. She, however, expressed neither

---

[11] In this context, a ceremony to ward off the evil eye.

shock nor disappointment. On the contrary, she smilingly welcomed her co-wife. Was she not after all brought up in the best traditions of Indian womanhood? After all, did not Sage Kanva advise Shakuntala to serve with love the elders at her husband's family and maintain cordial relations with his other wives?[12]

Seshadri Iyengar's second wife gave birth to a son. The celebrations that followed were lavish—more on the scale of a wedding. The child was named Srinivasa Raghavan and enjoyed the love and affection of his parents and stepmother. However, all this happiness was vouchsafed to the boy only for a short while. His mother died following a brief illness when he was just three. The obsequies had barely concluded when 12 days later, the senior wife of Seshadri Iyengar also died. The husband was shattered following these twin tragedies and remained homebound for a while.

But after a while, his sister and other relatives began advising him to get married again. He too, after considering that his young son needed a mother, consented, and married a third time.

Despite its status as the capital of a large estate, Ramanathapuram comprised little more than the palace, the Rajarajeswari Temple and a primary school. The district court, the collector's office, other administrative departments of the British, and the high schools were all located in Madurai. To further the education of

---

[12] A reference to *Abhijnana Shakuntalam*, a play by Kalidasa.

his only son, Seshadri Iyengar took the permission of the Setupati and moved to Madurai where he took up residence in a large house that he purchased at the Danappa Mudali Agraharam. From here, he would often travel to Ramanathapuram. The journey would be in an ivory-inlaid palanquin escorted by soldiers bearing revolvers, staves, spears and shields.

Meanwhile, the adoption case of the Setupati had moved in a leisurely fashion from the lower courts to the Madras High Court. It now required the services of a professional senior lawyer. Those were times when barristers were largely British. Sriman Seshadri Iyengar came to Madras to engage the services of the most famous of them all—Eardley Norton. But the latter had already committed to appear for the opponents, and he advised Seshadri Iyengar to hire the city's most famous vakil, Sir V. Bhashyam Iyengar.

Mylapore was where the senior vakils resided. Luz Church and Moubrays[13] Roads were where prominent figures in Madras society such as Baroda Dewan Srinivasa Iyengar[14], Judge Sir T. Madhav Row[15], Judge Sir T. Muthuswami Iyer[16], Rao Bahadur Ramachandra

---

[13] Today, T.T. Krishnamachari Road.

[14] Dewan Bahadur Srinivasa Raghava Iyengar was the dewan (prime minister) of Baroda State between 1896 and 1901.

[15] Sir Tanjore Madhav Row (1828–91) was dewan of three princely states—Travancore (1857–72), Indore (1873–75) and Baroda (1875–82). However, he was never a judge.

[16] The first Indian to become a judge of a High Court.

Saheb[17], Judge Sundaram Iyer[18], Dubash Buchi Babu, Chitti Babu[19], Sir K. Krishnaswami Iyer[20], Barrister N. Subramanyam[21] and C.R. Pattabhirama Iyer (father of Sir C.P. Ramaswami Iyer[22]) lived in large bungalows.

The Madras Presidency of those times was not the Madras State[23] of today which comprises 13 districts. Then, it included Andhra, parts of Kerala and Mysore, and was huge. The Andhra region had large estates such as Pithapuram, Venkatagiri, Bobbili, Nuzvid and Parlakimedi, and also native states such

---

[17] Rao Bahadur C. Ramachandra Rao Saheb was an early practitioner of law in the High Court and the first Indian to become Professor of Law at the Government Law College, Madras.

[18] Justice P.R. Sundara Iyer was a legal luminary of the late nineteenth and early twentieth centuries.

[19] Both Buchi Babu (real name Venkatamahipathi Naidu) and Chitti Babu were grandsons of Moddaverapu Dera Venkataswami Naidu, translator at Parry & Co. They were better known as sportspersons. Buchi Babu is considered the father of South Indian cricket, for he funded the entry of natives into the game at a time when it was a British preserve.

[20] V. (not K.) Krishnaswami Iyer (not knighted either), though he was conferred the CIE by the King in 1905. A legal luminary who became vakil, Judge and then Member of the Governor's Executive Council, he is remembered today as an institution builder and philanthropist. The Indian Bank, the Madras Sanskrit College and the Mylapore Club were all his creations.

[21] Dewan Bahadur N. Subramanyam was Advocate General, Government of Madras. A convert to Christianity, the C.S.I. Kalyani Hospital in Mylapore was set up at his behest and named after his mother.

[22] A brilliant, if controversial, lawyer who later became dewan of Travancore State.

[23] Renamed Tamil Nadu in 1968.

as Vizianagaram. The Tamil areas had principalities such as Ramanathapuram, Sivaganga, Oothukuzhi, Bodinayakanur and Singampatti, besides landowning religious establishments such as Thiruvavaduturai, Thirupananthal, Dharumapuram and Kunrakkudi. All of these would invariably have some case or the other coming up in the Madras High Court, and it was Sir V. Bhashyam Iyengar who regularly represented them. Other famous lawyers would argue on behalf of the opponents. Besides these, the mercantile community of Chettiars that had extensive money-lending activities in Rangoon, Singapore, Malaya and Ceylon employed Bhashyam Iyengar as their vakil. In his knowledge of law and for arguing on the Original side[24] of the Madras High Court, he was considered nonpareil.

---

[24] The High Court was divided between the Original and Appellate sides. The former dealt with fresh litigations, while the latter focused on appeals on judgements passed earlier.

2

The Vembakkam Clan

Vembakkam is a small village in the Chengalput District, about three miles from Singaperumal Koil. In it lived a Brahmin family that had migrated from the north. Once, senior police official Sri Raghavachariar, after whom a street is named in North Madras[25], was camping at Vembakkam. He became very friendly with the head of this family. The latter had a son who was highly intelligent. Impressed with his personality and communication skills, Raghavachariar offered to take care of his future and requested that the boy be sent to Madras with him.

Sir V. Bhashyam Iyengar

The boy endeared himself to everyone in Raghavachariar's family and acquitted himself well. He studied diligently, and eventually, on graduation, found employment as well. Raghavachariar got his daughter married to the

---

[25]Police Raghavachariar Square no longer exists.

boy; they had a daughter and three sons. The eldest son practised as a vakil in Mettupalayam, a place close to Saidapet, Madras, while the youngest became a judge at a district court. The second son, having earned a BA degree, wanted to study law. But family circumstances did not allow for such expenditure. He, therefore, found employment as a sub-registrar in Kumbakonam. Over the course of time, he was married to Ambujavalli, the second daughter of the Tahsildar of Ponneri.

Even while working as a sub-registrar, he qualified in law and set up practice as a vakil in Madras. The world soon noticed his skills. This was none other than Sir V. Bhashyam Iyengar.

V.C. Desikachariar

Ambujavalli's eldest sister was named Periamma. Her husband was a dubash[26] in Madras. Their only daughter Akkaiyya was married to V.C. Desikachari. He too was a famed vakil in Madras and was greatly interested in social work. He was the founder of the Madras State Co-operative Bank[27]. His son-in-law K. Bhashyam was also a prominent vakil. Being interested in politics, he joined the Congress Party and was imprisoned during

---

[26]'Dubash' or 'dvi bhashi' literally means 'one who knows two languages'. These interpreters/translators were much in demand during the British rule.

[27]Now the Tamil Nadu State Apex Co-Operative Bank Limited; founded in 1905, it was India's first co-operative bank.

the freedom struggle. Later, he was a member of the Prakasam cabinet[28].

V.C. Seshachariar

He was the younger brother of V.C. Desikachariar and an ardent disciple of Annie Besant and H.S. Olcott. He was, therefore, an ardent Theosophist, involved in causes championed by Besant.

V.V. Srinivasa Iyengar

Even though he practised as a vakil, he was a very orthodox man, particular about all religious practices. He participated with gusto in matters concerning literature, music and theatre. A kinsman of Police Raghavachariar, he too came from Vembakkam to Madras.

V.C. Gopalratnam

V.C. Desikachariar's son, he too became a famous lawyer. A prolific author of humorous stories and articles, he acted in numerous plays of Rao Bahadur Pammal Sambanda Mudaliar[29]. He was, therefore, an active member of the

---

[28] The 1946 Legislative Assembly elections in Madras Presidency saw a short-lived Congress government, led by T. Prakasam.

[29] Considered the father of modern Tamil theatre, Pammal Sambanda Mudaliar was the founder of the Suguna Vilasa Sabha, at one time a high-profile social organization dedicated to staging plays.

Suguna Vilasa Sabha, now located on Mount Road. He was married to V.V. Srinivasa Iyengar's daughter.

V.T. Lakshmi Ammal

Sir V. Bhashyam Iyengar's younger brother was, as mentioned earlier, a district judge. Lakshmi Ammal was his daughter's daughter. Having lost her husband early in life and being childless, she immersed herself in social work, especially the emancipation of women. She retired after having served as Superintendent of the Vigilance Home for several years.

The Mysore Dewan

Sir V. Bhashyam Iyengar's sister was married to Sri Rangacharlu of Bangalore. The latter worked initially in a senior position in the Madras Secretariat and was greatly respected by the British for his intelligence and efficiency. He was, therefore, appointed as the dewan of Mysore, in succession to Dewan Purniah. Sri Rangacharlu was the first dewan of the princely state of Mysore[30].

Sir V. Bhashyam Iyengar had four sons and six daughters. He conducted the wedding of his first son. Like the father, this boy too qualified in law when he was 20. But just before he was registered as a vakil at the

---

[30]Ambujammal is not correct in this—a century separated Purniah and Rangacharlu, with several dewans in between.

High Court, he suffered from excruciating stomach pain and passed away. Sir V. Bhashyam Iyengar's second son was Rangaswami; he was a chief engineer in Bangalore. He worked tirelessly for the reconstruction of the Jewell water-filtering system[31] in that city. He also founded the first metal factory[32] and constructed the great bridge over the Krishna River.

Sir V. Bhashyam Iyengar initially resided at Lily Pond House in Mandaveli, on the outskirts of Mylapore. Unlike present times, Madras did not have boarding houses or 'lodges' on practically every street. Those from outside the city who had business with law courts would invariably stay with their lawyers. Lily Pond House proved inadequate for such purposes. Sir V. Bhashyam Iyengar, therefore, purchased Lakshmi Vilas, a bungalow on the eastern end of Luz Church Road, Mylapore, modified it to suit his needs, and shifted there.

It was in that residence that his fifth daughter, Ranganayaki was born. In keeping with the adage that a fifth daughter is lucky, she remained so throughout her life. Ranganayaki's elder sister was Seethamma. She was married to Kumbakonam C.R. Thiruvenkatachariar, who had qualified in law and begun life as an apprentice under Sir V. Bhashyam Iyengar. Before he could rise to great

---

[31] A Jewell water filter was a system of sand filters for filtering and treating water for drinking purposes that made use of gravity to allow water to percolate through a column of sand inside cylindrical cisterns that was widely used in the early twentieth century.

[32] The Premier Metal Factory at Mandya.

heights in the profession, the government appointed him a judge at the City Civil Court. He was, nevertheless, referred to as Judge Thiruvenkatachari. He built Sita Vilas, a bungalow at Luz Corner, and resided there. The State Bank of India operates from the premises now.

Sir V. Bhashyam Iyengar's second daughter was married to Rangamani Iyengar of Tirunelveli. The son Rangaswami, who was an engineer, was wedded to a girl from Thiruvallikeni, and the son who came next was married to Dewan Rangacharlu's daughter's daughter.

Having appointed Sir V. Bhashyam Iyengar as the vakil to argue for the Ramanathapuram Estate, Sriman Seshadri Iyengar had to often visit Madras. His son Srinivasa Raghavan was then 12, and studying at the Madurai Setupati High School. His academic record was brilliant, and he invariably stood first in all the annual examinations. His father doted on him and could not bear to be separated from him even for a short while. When the Ramanathapuram case hearing was going on in the High Court, Seshadri Iyengar would stay for days on end at Sir V. Bhashyam Iyengar's house in Madras. His son would invariably accompany him. The children of the Bhashyam Iyengar household rejoiced in Srinivasa Raghavan's company. They shortened his name to Cheema, and that became Maasi later. They would celebrate his arrival, claiming that the son-in-law from Madurai had come.

Sir V. Bhashyam Iyengar's daughter Ranganayaki was then five. Light skinned and slim, blessed with abundant hair that threatened to be unruly, she would be playing around, clad in a skirt and top. It is but natural that discussions and parleys that happen in the residences of the rich and famous become grist for gossip mills. In keeping with that, rumours began to circulate that Ranganayaki was engaged to be married to Srinivasa Raghavan. When these tales reached Madurai and Ramanathapuram, Seshadri Iyengar's relatives, in particular, a cousin who lived in Kakkaithoppu[33], expressed stern opposition.

She, therefore, arrived one day to voice her disapproval. In her view, Cheema had to marry a suitable girl from Ramanathapuram and nowhere else. She argued at length with Seshadri Iyengar, who having heard her out, simply said that Cheema desired to marry only the Madras girl and none else. He also advised his cousin to verify this with the boy directly. He too was present, and the lady immediately moved over to him and asked, 'What is this, Cheema? In what way is that Madras girl superior? If you so desire, I will bring a hundred girls from Kakkaithoppu and line them up before you to take your pick. Don't marry this girl from the vile city.'

To this, Cheema simply replied that if he ever married, it would be only to the city girl.

The wedding of Srinivasa Raghavan and Ranganayaki was celebrated in a grand manner over five days at Lakshmi Vilas. The formal entry of the bride into her

---

[33] A part of Madurai town.

husband's home was observed at Madurai. The entire town marvelled at the trousseau Sir V. Bhashyam Iyengar had provided. There are people who remember even now the way in which the gifts were borne in a procession that stretched to the end of Danappa Mudali Agraharam. Srinivasa Raghavan was then 14 and Ranganayaki seven.

The Ramanathapuram case verdict when delivered was a resounding victory for the Setupati. The ruler's joy knew no bounds. He praised Sir V. Bhashyam Iyengar, and as for Seshadri Iyengar, who had been the prime mover, he was gifted Thiruthervalai, a sub-zamin comprising 18 villages. From then on, he was referred to as the Thiruthervalai Zamindar. Srinivasa Raghavan cleared his matriculation examination, standing first in his school. Madurai did not have any colleges then, so it was decided that he would stay at his father-in-law's house in Madras and enrol in an institution there. However much he delighted in his son becoming a graduate, Zamin Seshadri Iyengar was keen that he should not abandon the orthodox traditions of his community. A cook who adhered to all such mores was hired, and he accompanied Srinivasa Raghavan to Madras.

Let us start referring to Srinivasa Raghavan as Srinivasan from now on. His father-in-law doted on him, but the young man never allowed the boundaries of propriety to be crossed. He did not take advantage of the affection showered on him, nor did he begin taking liberties with his in-laws. He remained essentially focused on his studies.

The Vembakkam Clan

Cheema wanted to sit for the ICS examination, but his father did not desire it. It involved the candidate going to England[34], and Seshadri Iyengar could not bear a long separation from his son. Moreover, he did not want his son to break with tradition and cross the seas[35]. Srinivasan was, therefore, advised to study law and set up practice like his father-in-law. Accordingly, having completed his BA at the Presidency College, Madras, he joined the Law College. Ranganayaki and he set up home at Palathope Street in Mylapore, in a house that belonged to Sir V. Bhashyam Iyengar. Ranganayaki was then 13, and Srinivasan was 20.

Madras of the late nineteenth century was not the city we know now. People lived in the densely packed Kothawal Chawdi area in the northern part of the city. The locality was referred to as Black Town by the white-skinned rulers. They considered it beneath their dignity to live in that area as it was populated by people whom they labelled 'blacks'. They chose instead to reside in south Madras. Let us now see how that part of the city functioned.

Then and now, Madras was, and is, a quiet city. In particular, south Madras of those days was gripped by an eerie silence. There were no motor horns and noisy buses, nor were there bright lights to dazzle the eyes. When the sun set, the roads turned into dark caves, and nobody ventured out. Certain areas of south Madras such

---

[34] It was only from 1922 that the exams were held in India as well.
[35] In the nineteenth century, Hindus could not cross the ocean without losing their caste.

as Mylapore, Alwarpet, Teynampet and Mambalam were filled with clumps of tall bamboo, Madras thorn and mesquite trees, and looked like small forests.

There was yet another reason for south Madras appearing so empty. There were hardly any residents or houses. People would hesitate to cross the backwater channel in Mylapore and come to the Luz Church or Kattukoil (literally 'temple in the forest') area even during the day, let alone at night. Hardly anyone would stir out after 6.00 p.m. Luz Church was in such a dark locality. On either side of the road, Madras thorn, rain trees, banyan and peepal grew abundantly, even as bamboos flourished as thickets. The thoroughfare leading to Kattukoil was known as Luz Church Road.

Sometime in the past, a Portuguese ship was sailing towards Madras when a storm threatened it. The night was dark and the sea rough—it seemed as though the vessel would capsize. The sailors knelt on the deck and prayed to their tutelary deity, Virgin Mary. A light appeared on the western horizon, and they could see the San Thome seashore very clearly. The storm began to subside. The sailors began moving towards the light and arrived at the San Thome beach. The light, however, did not stop moving and kept heading westwards. The sailors followed it enthusiastically. At a particular point, the light vanished, and the sailors decided to erect a church for the Virgin at that spot. They called it Luz Church (Luz means 'light' in Portuguese). The residents of Madras, however, referred to it as Kattukoil.

The Vembakkam Clan

The British and the Portuguese began to settle on the Luz Church and Moubrays roads. They built huge bungalows on both sides of the roads. Banana plantations, fields and tanks occupied the remaining spaces. We can see a bungalow named Sudder Gate even now on Moubrays Road[36]. This was once the law court of the East India Company[37]. Over time, some of the top-ranking lawyers of Mylapore purchased these bungalows and moved in. One of these was the bungalow that stands even now behind Kamadhenu Theatre[38]. This was Lakshmi Vilas.

The Tamil month of Margazhi (December/January) is best known for its chill and dew. The weather then was not what it is now; it would be mildly cold even during the day. Villagers and townspeople would go around wearing woollen caps with earmuffs morning and evening. The rich who went around in carriages would wear caps and mufflers.

Sundays being holidays would be quieter than usual.

It was in such silence that on Sunday, 8 January 1899, the palatial Lakshmi Vilas witnessed a great commotion. Ambujavalli, Lady Bhashyam Iyengar, was waiting impatiently. She was dressed in a wide-bordered saree

---

[36] Sudder Gate survived well into the twenty-first century but was demolished to make way for a high-rise. It served as Ambujammal's residence as well in later years.

[37] The eighteenth century saw the establishment of the Sudder Dewani Adalat, which was the court for civil cases.

[38] Kamadhenu Theatre was a marriage hall till recently and is now slated for demolition, but Lakshmi Vilas vanished a long while ago.

and wearing several pieces of diamond jewellery. Within a short while, the cry of a newborn baby was heard and then the commotion ceased. The midwife emerged from the labour room and announced that it was 'only' a girl. Lady Bhashyam Iyengar's face registered disappointment. Almost unconsciously she gave vent to her frustration: 'Could this not have been a boy? Who asked for a girl?' She felt cheated that her daughter Ranganayaki had not delivered a son.

And then, having regained control over her emotions, she declared that her daughter Ranganayaki being the fifth girl was lucky, and hoped that the newborn would also be fortunate. Even as she uttered this benediction, her husband Sir V. Bhashyam Iyengar arrived. Tall and built big, he looked his usual regal self—a spotless white dhoti worn in the traditional style, a long alpaca coat, turban, diamond studs in the ears, and the Vaishnavite mark on his forehead.

His arrival coincided with the midwife emerging from the labour room again. She clearly lost her nerve on seeing him, and eager to protect herself from any of the blame for having brought forth a girl, she declared that the infant was clearly a boy at birth and had miraculously become a girl later. Everyone laughed on hearing such nonsense. Her work done, the lady doctor too came out. Sir V. Bhashyam Iyengar enquired if the mother and child were doing well.

'The delivery was smooth,' she replied. 'But the mother is very weak. She did not even look at the baby.

She needs rest and nobody should disturb her.' Having said this, she took her leave.

This was Ranganayaki's third delivery. She was constitutionally weak and would faint often. Her first child was a girl that died in its tenth month. The second too was a girl. She was quite confident that her third would be a boy and, therefore, she was quite frustrated that this too was a girl. This led to her disliking the child from the start.

It was an old belief that if you named a girl after her maternal grandmother, the succeeding babies would all be boys. Based on this, the elders in the family named the newborn Ambujavalli. It is that Ambujavalli, whose name was considered too long by Gandhiji, and therefore shortened by him to Ambujam, who is now relating to you her story!

Mother Ranganayaki's health never improved after the birth of Ambujavalli. She did not have enough milk to feed her child. Moreover, the doctors opined that if the baby drank the mother's milk, it would become weak. A wet nurse was, therefore, brought in from the village. Despite feeding from this woman, the baby's health did not improve. Sores erupted all over her and she became emaciated. It was at this time that Ranganayaki's second daughter fell ill with typhoid and died within 10 days. This shock further weakened Ranganayaki, and whenever she saw her surviving child, she would berate her for having brought about the death of her older sibling.

'I detest this child with its sores and incessant crying!'

she declared. 'I hate her very sight. I don't want her. Let someone else bring her up.' Ranganayaki's younger sister Kalyani offered to take on the responsibility. The child, therefore, was brought to Lakshmi Vilas where Kalyani lived. A senior doctor was brought in to examine her, and he declared that she needed to be shifted to a cooler climate for her health to improve.

Sir V. Bhashyam Iyengar organized for the baby to be sent to his son Rangaswami's house in Bangalore, in the company of a Eurasian nurse. A complete cure was affected in 10 months, and the child was sent back. Gone were the sores and the sunken stomach. The girl was now healthy and looked good. Why, even the mother who had professed to be disgusted with her now became affectionate.

In April 1901, Ranganayaki delivered her fourth child. Madurai Sriman Seshadri Iyengar and Madras Sir V. Bhashyam Iyengar were delighted that it was a boy. The two grandfathers declared in one voice that he would be named Parthasarathy.

Srinivasa Iyengar, who had thus far been a junior to his father-in-law Sir V. Bhashyam Iyengar in legal practice, progressed rapidly in his career. Others such as his brother-in-law C.R. Thiruvenkatachari and Mylapore vakil Gopalaswami Iyengar became his juniors; his client list increased by the day. The Palathope house was no longer sufficient, and he shifted with family to a large double-storeyed house belonging to his father-in-law, on Mylapore's North Mada Street.

3

My Childhood Memories

I CANNOT SAY THAT EVERYTHING THAT HAPPENED IN MY childhood remains etched in my memory. But I do recall that my brother and I were brought up with a lot of affection.

These days, parents celebrate every birthday of their children. My brother and I, however, never had our birthdays celebrated with feasts or new clothes. But I do recall that each year, on the asterism of my brother's birth, Amma would send someone to offer special worship at the Kesava Perumal Temple. Parents of that era considered daughters to be less important, compared to their sons. Since they were eventually to be married off and would belong to another household, girls had no rights or privileges.

My brother and I were very close. Even though several incidents took place when we were young, a particular one stands out in my memory. I was five and he, two years younger. Our Mylapore North Mada Street house was really big and comprised three quadrangles, arranged one after another, leading eventually to Palathope at the rear.

There were servants' quarters and a vegetable garden at the back. Jackfruit and coconut trees also grew there in abundance. There were three wells—the first in the garden, the second in the central courtyard, and the third in the kitchen. Potable water would be brought in huge cauldrons by bullock carts all the way from the Tiruvanmiyur Marundeeswarar Temple tank. There was no piped water supply in the city.

One morning at around 10, Amma finished feeding my brother, and having completed rinsing his hands at the well in the backyard, went back with him into the house. I, for some reason, stayed back at the well. All of a sudden, one of the cows in our backyard broke free from its tether and charged. It was a huge Nellore cow. It must have been enraged by my red silk skirt. I screamed, terrified. On hearing my cry, Amma rushed out, and gathering me in her arms, lifted me up to seat me at her waist. But the cow did not give up. It now began to chase her.

Amma ran round and round the well. Even as we ran and the cow chased us, our cowherd arrived as if by divine providence. The cow immediately quietened down and returned on its own to its shed. If, on hearing my scream, Amma had not rushed out and carried me, unmindful of the risk to her, I would have been killed. After so many years, I still occasionally have nightmares of being chased by a cow.

At night, we demanded stories from Amma. We would refuse to go to bed if she did not consent to relate some tale or the other. Thus, every night, we would have some story or the other. One of these was about a demon who, in order to become invincible, had stored his life in a small container that he then hid in the stomach of a bee, which lived in a tree's hollow. Having heard this, the conversation between us two children for the next few days revolved around the demon, his life, the container, the bee and the tree hollow. We then came to a conclusion.

We located two cane sticks in our house and placed them before the idols of gods that we played with. We then play-acted a worship for all of these, and then imagined that our lives were now safely stored inside the two cane sticks. And then? We became bold and confident that no one could get the better of us. We boasted about what we had done to all our playmates. We kept the two cane sticks well-hidden. At night, we would retrieve them and keep them below our beds.

Around six o'clock one evening, the two of us were playing in the central courtyard. The servants were all in the backyard, busy with their work. The growing darkness frightened us. I can still recall what my brother said in a baby's lisp: 'Akka! Our parents are not here. We are abandoned. Let us both lament our condition, or at least pray to God.' A lantern hung from the rafters in the courtyard. The boy who came from the shop opposite to light this each evening had not reached our home. This was why we were afraid.

My brother and I played at many things in those days.

An important pastime was the building of temples and their chariots. We would thus enact Vinayaka Chaturthi, Krishna Jayanthi and other such festivals. The shrines would be fashioned out of sticks and books, and the idols would be placed inside them. The celebrations would go on for 10 days.

Even though this was all make-believe, certain aspects were for real. Children from the neighbourhood would come to worship at our temple. Our mother would make arrangements for sweetmeats and other offerings to the deities. I am not sure if either we siblings or the other children were really devoted to the gods! But we were devoted to the food offerings for sure.

When young, I was often branded as adamant and argumentative. In contrast, my brother, was submissive, and so considered a good child. Thus, when it came to the weekly oil massage and bath, I would protest. My mother would brandish the grip of the hand fan and approach me—I would hide in my father's office.

Lakshmi Vilas was just like a palace. It had two wings— in one was the kitchen, the puja room and the ladies' quarters, the other functioned as my grandfather's office. This was where his juniors, including his sons and sons-in-law, worked. At night, everyone including grandfather slept on the upper floor.

Fronting the bungalow was a lovely pond with steps on all four sides leading to the water. A statue of Sri Krishna stood in its middle. On full and new moon days, and on the 11th day of the lunar cycle, women from the household and those of the neighbourhood would bathe in this pond. On other days, we would just gaze at the Krishna idol and the lotuses that blossomed around it and rejoice at the sight. The beauty of the lotus pond is etched indelibly in my mind.

In the courtyard that linked the two wings was a large mango tree. It had spread to form a canopy. My grandfather had gotten a swing tied to a branch of the tree. This was where we grandchildren played.

Our father was very strict. We had to seek his permission even before going to our grandfather's house. A servant would escort us there at 4 p.m. and get us back at 6 p.m. On certain evenings, the other grandchildren would go to the People's Park[39] but because we did not have our father's permission, we would stay back.

Grandfather Bhashyam Iyengar doted on us. He considered us to be model children as we obeyed our father implicitly. He would recline in the evenings in an easy chair at the entrance of the bungalow. Clad in coat and turban, he was dignity personified. Those days, he was a judge of the High Court[40]. Standing by his side would be his liveried and turbaned peon. Grandfather would address him: 'Hey Munusami, go get

---

[39]People's Park was a huge green lung of the city located near the Central Station. It has now all but vanished, its space having been consumed by extensions to the railway, the stadium, Ripon Buildings and the Victoria Public Hall.

[40]Elevated as Judge of the High Court in 1901, he resigned in 1904 to continue practising as a lawyer till his passing in 1908.

the children almonds and raisins.' In those days, where were chocolates and biscuits?

Every evening, a golden tumbler filled with milk laced with saffron and edible camphor would be brought for Grandfather. I would secretly want to drink milk from a gold tumbler but never had the courage to express this before Grandfather. All my bravado was limited to my talks with my grandmother.

She would be seated on the stone platform outside the kitchen, sorting something or the other. I would seat myself on a three-legged stool and chat with her. It was customary for us grandchildren to address our grandfather as Iya and our grandmother as Iyamma, respectively. On one occasion, I asked my grandmother: 'Why, Iyamma, do you wear so much jewellery when you have grown so old and your hair so grey? If you gave them to me, I could wear them.'

Everyone present, including my grandmother, burst into laughter. 'Look at my Ambujavalli! How smart she is!' she remarked. The news reached Bhashyam Iyengar, and he reacted like a typical lawyer: 'Oho! Has Ambujavalli already staked her claim to a share of her grandmother's jewellery?' I would, however, not give in. 'Can an old woman wear so much jewellery?' I persisted. 'That is why I asked for them.' Thus, I was branded as argumentative.

Grandmother was bedecked in jewellery of that age. She wore bangles, earrings, nose rings and a waistband; they were all studded with diamonds. She would routinely wear them every morning and remove them at night.

She always wore Bangalore silk with a double brocade border. We never knew her to speak or laugh loudly, grow perturbed, or walk rapidly. She resembled an ivory figurine and walked slowly. Hers was an indescribable dignity that ensured that everyone—adults and children—loved her, yet remained somewhat in awe of her.

At times, Grandmother would mix rice with *rasam* or buttermilk and feed us, giving each of us a ball of the preparation in our palms. It was delicious and we would keep asking for more till we had stuffed ourselves. We would suffer agonies, thereafter. Grandmother was a devout and orthodox woman who dedicated her life to the service of her husband.

Grandfather Bhashyam Iyengar led the life of an aristocrat. The house always had rulers, zamindars and other prominent members of society as visitors. Besides them, there were also relatives and poor supplicants. Welcoming all varieties of guests and taking care of their requirements was an important part of my grandmother's duties.

Lady Bhashyam Iyengar also had to often attend banquets and garden tea parties that the government hosted. She participated in public functions and also presided at prize distributions. She would address such gatherings in Tamil, and a translation in English would be read out subsequently. At her behest, and with Sir V. Bhashyam Iyengar's encouragement, Madras city saw three entities of public benefit being set up. In order to make up for the lack of a school for girls, Sir V. Bhashyam

Iyengar convinced the Maharaja of Vizianagaram to sponsor the founding of the National Girls' High School. This functions as the Lady Sivaswami Iyer High School[41].

Realizing that there was no hospital dedicated to women's health, Lady Bhashyam Iyengar, with great effort, obtained government support and made arrangements for such an institution. It had an operation theatre and a private ward in her name. This facility is now known as the Gosha Hospital. It is officially named after Kasturba Gandhi[42].

A park exclusively for women was the third project, and it came up on the land next to the Ice House[43] on the Marina beachfront. This was named Lady Wenlock Park after the wife of the then Governor of Madras. A building housing a club for the entertainment of women who came to the beach was constructed in the middle of the park. Lady Bhashyam Iyengar and Lady Ramaswami Mudaliar, the wife of Raja Sir Savalai Ramaswami Mudaliar[44], strove to make this a reality.

---

[41] Known today as Lady Sivaswami Iyer Higher Secondary School, it is located on Sundareswarar Street, Mylapore.

[42] Known today as the Kasturba Gandhi Hospital for Women and Children, it was begun in 1885 as the Royal Victoria Caste & Gosha Hospital. Several leading women of Madras were involved in its inception, the prime mover being Mary Dacombe Scharlieb, the city's first lady doctor.

[43] Constructed in the 1840s to store ice imported from the United States of America, it is now a memorial to Swami Vivekananda.

[44] A leading businessman, philanthropist and sometimes, Sheriff of Madras.

It was the habit of Lady Bhashyam Iyengar to host discourses on the *Bhagavatam* and *Ramayana* and reward the scholars suitably. The first *Harikatha* recital by C. Saraswati Bai[45], who grew up in the Buchi Babu household[46], was held at Lakshmi Vilas. Similarly, the debut performance of Kadappai Lakshmi Ammal[47] was also held here, and my grandmother helped further her career in many ways.

Though she had many good qualities, I would sometimes classify my grandmother as hard-hearted. This was chiefly owed to her orthodoxy. Even if a child were to try embracing her, she would move away. 'You are ritually impure,' she would say. 'Stay clear.' Yet, when her husband returned from the High Court, she would wipe his feet clean and press them. There was no question of ritual impurity in his case.

When she met us, she never asked about our studies or how we were faring in them. Instead, she asked me if I was

---

[45]The first woman outside of the courtesan community to take to the performing arts, her debut and initial performances saw great protests from orthodox society. It is a wonder that for all her conservatism, Lady Bhashyam Iyengar thought it fit to host a performance by C. Saraswati Bai.

[46]As noted in the earlier chapter, Buchi Babu was a gentleman of leisure who did much to promote sports in Madras. The household had several families he took care of. C. Saraswati Bai's parents too were such beneficiaries.

[47]Like C. Saraswati Bai, Kadappai Lakshmi Ammal was also a pioneer among women outside of the courtesan community. But she was widowed early, so she did not have a long performing career.

learning the *pasurams*[48] and the *Thiruppavai*[49]. My brother would be asked if he was performing *sandhyavandanam*[50] thrice a day, and if he applied the sacred Vaishnavite mark on his forehead.

When Sir P. Rajagopalachariar[51] returned after a visit to England, my father hosted a dinner for him at our residence, Amjad Bagh[52]. On coming to know of it the next day, my grandmother sent for my mother and enquired: 'Is it true that your husband sat down to dinner with someone who had crossed the seas? Is this in line with our Vaishnava traditions? Hereafter I cannot accept even water from you.'

Grandfather Sir V. Bhashyam Iyengar had a routine each evening of setting out in a double-horse carriage

---

[48]Devotional or mystical poems, sacred to the Vaishnavite community, these are 4,000 in number, and form the works of the 12 canonical Vaishnavite saints—the Alwars

[49]A set of 30 verses that belong to the pasuram category, and that are very sacred to Vaishnavites, composed by Andal, the only eighth-century woman Alwar, and are usually sung in the month of Margazhi (December/January).

[50]A ritual to be performed thrice a day by all Brahmin males who sport the sacred thread.

[51]An administrator who was dewan (prime minister) successively of the princely states of Cochin and Travancore, he later became a member of the Governor's Council, Madras. He served in the Council of India, London, between 1923 and 1925, and Ambujammal is clearly talking of an event that happened much later in her life.

[52]While in this chapter Ambujammal was residing in North Mada Street, her father, soon to rise to the pinnacle of his career, later shifted residence to a sprawling bungalow called Amjad Bagh on Luz Church Road.

for the beach. He would come to our house on North Mada Street, and remaining seated in his carriage, call for my mother. Having conversed briefly with her, he would take us children to the beach. He would call at our house during his morning walk too. My father would not allow my mother to visit her parents' home frequently. He was a very strict man and short-tempered too. Since my mother could not go to her paternal home often, my grandfather made it a practice to call at our house. On festival days, however, we would all go to Lakshmi Vilas for our meals. On the day after the Pongal festival, the entire family, numbering around 60 people—adults and children included—would gather at the lotus pond at Lakshmi Vilas and feast on pongal (rice cooked in boiling milk), tamarind rice and curd rice, served on lotus leaves. These were occasions of great joy for all of us. Such dinners by the pond have now become a rarity.

4

Madurai Grandfather

Every summer my parents would take me to a hill station like Coonoor, Ootacamund or Kodaikanal because I would erupt in rashes in the heat of Madras. Many mocked me saying I was like an English girl. We always spent around 15 days in Madurai every time we returned from our stay in a hill station. My Madurai grandfather's Danappa Mudali Agraharam residence was a large house with three quadrangles. However, there were no women! Other than my grandfather, there was Venkatesan, the son by his third wife, and a few servants. Just three years separated Uncle Venkatesan and me! Even when I was a child, my step-grandmother, that is my grandfather's third wife, passed away. His elderly sister had died even earlier. Uncle Venkatesan was, therefore, entrusted to the care of servants.

Every day, my grandfather would eat only after worshipping the *salagrama*s[53] and reading the Ramayana. It was only after he had eaten that we were served our

---

[53]Ammonites that are considered representatives of Vishnu.

meals. He would relax in the reclining chair in the front courtyard and converse with those of his friends who lived nearby or who passed by. There was a horse carriage in my grandfather's house, and every evening, we would go to the Meenakshi Amman Temple in it.

Every morning, Grandfather would sit in his strongroom and count cash after closing the door. We would hear the sound of the coins jingling and bang on the door, asking to be let in, but nothing would disturb him. He would jokingly reply that he would open the door only when we left for Madras.

On the day of our departure from Madurai, Grandfather would gift my mother a *sungudi*[54] saree and give me a sungudi skirt. He was not the kind of man who would indulge his grandchildren and buy all kinds of gifts. The elders of that generation were nearly all like this.

When he visited us in Madras, he would bring a tin of ghee, a bag of Decalepis root[55], a sack of dried wild melon and small green mangoes. As soon as he arrived, Lady Bhashyam Iyengar would come to see him. She would bring rice, lentils and all other provisions in trays and fill the entire central quadrangle of our house. My orthodox grandfather would not eat in anybody else's house, so instead of inviting him to her home, Lakshmi

---

[54] Cotton textile unique to Madurai, and reflecting Saurashtrian influence in its tie-and-dye designs.
[55] Known as Mahalikizhangu, and made into a pickle, its strong odour makes it an acquired taste.

Vilas, she would bring all these provisions to our house.

When Grandfather returned to Madurai, my mother would send packets of special betel nuts, turmeric and asafoetida from Ramanujam Chetty's shop, along with his luggage, because these condiments were not available in Madurai. Grandfather would be ready at 3.00 p.m. for a train that left at 8! He would be in a lace-bordered dhoti worn in the traditional style, a silk shirt, an alpaca coat, a lace-bordered drape and a red brocade shawl from Kashmir. Diamond studs would flash from his ears, and the Vaishnavite mark would adorn his forehead. In his hand was a walking stick, and on his feet, slip-on shoes made fashionable by Muslim aristocracy. A lace-bordered turban completed his attire.

On his tin trunk would be a bedroll wrapped in a woollen blanket. One attendant would carry his puja box, wrapped in silk; another would carry his silver water carafe. His other luggage would be placed in the horse carriage. The children and servants would all assemble in the courtyard to see him off. My mother would be at the kitchen door. Father would be perusing his case files in the office room.

Uncle Venkatesan hated parting from us. He invariably hid somewhere at the time of departure, but in vain; the servants located him, anyway. He would weep and wail. We would take turns to fall at Grandfather's feet, and he would sprinkle sanctified rice grains on us and give us each a rupee. The servants would all be rewarded suitably. He would then take leave of Father who, in response, would ask Grandfather to intimate his safe arrival at Madurai by means of a letter. Uncle would then tearfully bid us all goodbye. We would immediately begin counting the days for his next visit.

Polio struck my brother when he was five. Despite several native treatments, there was no improvement. Finally, my parents consulted Dr Browning, an allopath. He placed the leg in a splint and tied bags of sand around it. He also recommended complete bed rest. My brother remained that way for a year. My parents and grandfathers prayed to all the gods for his speedy recovery. My brother, though just five, was equally devout. Each new moon day, special worship was offered to Lord Veeraraghava, the presiding deity at Tiruvallur. Sacred water would be brought from there, and only after partaking of it would he eat. There were no bus facilities to Tiruvallur those days; those who brought the offerings came by train and reached our home only in the evening. My brother fasted till then.

Venkatachalapati, the God at Tirumala, was the tutelary deity on my paternal side. Once my grandfather suffered seriously from an inflammation of the pharynx, and he decided to go to Tirumala by foot. While the women of the family and the luggage travelled by bullock cart, he walked. The only refreshments he had on the way were basil leaves, water, fruit and milk. When they returned, he was completely cured. If anybody in my house fell ill, my father would immediately pray to Tirumala and tie a rupee coin in turmeric-dyed cloth. This would later be offered at the shrine. By the grace of God and the treatment given by Dr Browning, my brother recovered, though for the rest of his life he had a slight limp.

My Education

When my brother was seven, he was admitted to the P.S. High School in Mylapore. As was customary then, this was done to the accompaniment of pipes, drums and an array of gifts from his maternal grandfather. There was no such formal ceremony for me. In those days, nobody celebrated ear-piercing or the formal initiation ceremonies of girls. There was no school exclusively meant for girls either, so I was never admitted to any educational institution[56]. I was taught at home by women from the Indian Missionary Society. The lessons would begin with a half-hour session on the Bible, and then we would get on with Tamil, maths and English. There would be a change of teacher every six months. The new arrival would trash the teaching methods of her predecessor, and the lessons would start all over again from the beginning. These women were very clever. They would relate the story of Jesus Christ in a very moving manner. When it got to the part about his having to wear a crown of thorns and being crucified, I would weep.

---

[56] Ambujammal is not entirely correct in this—the Vizianagaram Maharajah's Hindu Girls School, presently the Lady Sivaswami Iyer Girls Higher Secondary School, was functioning in Mylapore since 1869.

Immediately the teacher would say, 'See my child, how much Jesus suffered for the sake of mankind? Have any of your Gods undergone such privations?'

In those days, children from affluent Indian households were raised like their English counterparts. Thus, my brother and I always wore socks and shoes when we went out. My brother wore velvet shorts, a shirt and a cap for outings. I learnt riding when young. I would sit side-saddle and the trainer would lead me, holding the bridle. I never rode at a gallop. It was more a sedate trot all around the Mylapore Tank. My brother, owing to his leg, was not permitted to ride.

My mother's eldest sister Sitamma was married to C.R. Thiruvenkatachari, who was a judge in the Small Causes Court. They lived at Sita Vilas, the bungalow that was just opposite Lakshmi Vilas. Thiruvenkatachari's younger brother, Kumbakonam Lakshmiraghava Iyengar, was also a well-known personality. Thiruvenkatachari and Sitamma had six daughters and four sons. My mother's second oldest sister was Jayamma, and her husband Rangamani Iyer was the agent of a bank, and was hence referred to as the 'Bank Son-in-Law'. He was from Sevvalai in the Tirunelveli District and lived with his family at Lakshmi Vilas. Jayamma and Rangamani Iyengar's daughter Kalpakam and I were the same age. She was referred to as Kappu. Since I was given my grandmother's name, nobody called me by it. Instead, I was referred to as Pappi. My parents called me Pappamma or Pappu, and my brother Parthasarathy was referred to as Paccha.

Kappu and I were inseparable from infancy. Every day, after my brother had gone to school, the two of us would play. The Navaratri[57] celebrations were very grand at my home. Every evening, my mother would dress us up as Rama, Krishna or the *gopi*s and send us out to invite the ladies of the neighbouring houses. My brother would don a girl's outfit, and I that of a boy.

Natesa Iyer was engaged to teach us vocal music and the violin. He also taught the daughter of Justice P.R. Sundara Iyer and the daughters of Justice V. Krishnaswami Iyer. I would catch a cold easily, so I could not sing. Therefore, I was taught the violin while Kappu sang. The music tutor charged Rs 20 a month, which people considered very high. I must say that it was my mother who learnt more than I of what was taught. She would prompt me when I forgot some of the lines. Mother would never leave us alone with the music master. She would draw up a reclining chair and watch us from near the doorstep.

At the behest of my father, my mother learnt English and also to play the piano. A Eurasian lady was engaged to teach her. Amma learnt to play the piano very well, but for some unfathomable reason, I always felt sad when she played.

---

[57] The festival of nine nights celebrating the triumph of the goddess over evil. Households would display dolls and invite ladies from the neighbourhood to visit.

Janammal's Sad Fate

My mother's youngest sister was Janammal, just six years my senior. Her life was a sad one. She married the son of Rama Iyengar, a former dewan of Travancore who lived in Egmore. Even now, there is a road named after him in that area. The feelers for such a match came from the dewan's family when Janammal was five. Initially, my grandparents were reluctant to get such a young child married, but they were eventually charmed by the prospective in-laws and gave in.

As her husband's family lived in the same city, Janammal would be sent for quite frequently, and she repeatedly refused. Eventually, she would be forcibly sent, with a nurse. Having stayed there for a few days, she would return. Her husband qualified in law and served as an apprentice under my maternal grandfather. He was a big-built man, and swarthy of complexion.

When Janammal turned 14, she was sent to her in-laws' house, but she did not live there for even a year. One day, her husband stepped out and never returned. Search parties looked for him everywhere. Four months later, he was found in another town as a convert to Christianity. Sir V. Bhashyam Iyengar sent for him but he refused to come, stating that his wife could instead go back to her parental home. An enraged Bhashyam Iyengar declared that his daughter would henceforth not have anything to do with a Christian convert. Within six months, Janammmal's husband died of a fever. I mentioned that my eldest aunt Sita Thiruvenkatachari had six daughters. Janammal, in effect, became the seventh, and was cared for and protected by her eldest sister thereafter.

Sri S. Satyamurti

Having become an extremely successful vakil, my father had many apprentices and juniors. Among them, K. Soundararaja Iyengar, K.V. Krishnaswami Iyer, K. Rajah Iyer, K. Bhashyam Iyengar and S. Duraiswami Iyer became very successful practitioners of law. My father travelled very often in connection with his cases. It was rare for him to stay 10 days at a stretch at home. On days when the courts were closed, Father's close friends V.C. Seshachariar, Narayana Iyer, Ayyavayyar, and others would come home to play cards. I must add that they never gambled. My mother served them tea every half hour.

My father was fond of billiards and would go to play at the Mylapore Club every evening, returning by 9 p.m. Later, the billiards table we had at home, together with the piano Amma played on, were donated to the Lady Willingdon Club in Egmore[58].

S. Satyamurti[59], an active member of the Congress, was

---

[58]Officially known as the Egmore Ladies Recreation Club, it was located on Willingdon Estate and had Lady Willingdon as its powerful patroness, when she was the First Lady of Madras Presidency.

[59]S. Satyamurti (1887–1943) was a powerful orator and an engaging personality. The Mayor of Madras in 1939/1940, he was the man who envisaged the Poondy Reservoir, which today supplies so much water to the city. It is aptly named after him as Satyamurti Sagar.

my father's close friend and devoted to him. They met and chatted at least once every day. In case he did not visit, a car would be sent to fetch Satyamurti. If, despite this, there was a delay in his coming, my father would fume. 'Fool! Rascal! How long is he keeping me waiting,' he would shout and lose his temper at anyone who happened to be around. Just then, Satyamurti would arrive, asking in a loud voice: 'What, Srinivasa Iyengar? Why did you send for me?' On hearing his voice, my father's anger would vanish at once. 'What is this, Satyamurti? I sent for you a while ago,' my father would say in welcome. Both would then start talking animatedly. All of a sudden, loud arguments would erupt. Then they would resume in normal voices, and so it would go on. We would watch in wonder.

Uncle's Marriage

My uncle Venkatesa Iyengar was married to Pattammal, the second daughter of K. Srinivasa Iyengar, a prominent vakil residing on Luz Church Road. My mother filled in for the absence of a mother at his wedding. I was asked to tie the knot—a duty usually performed by the bridegroom's sister. My Madurai grandfather brought 50 Brahmins and 50 aged ladies along with him for the wedding. They were all from Sivaganga, Ramanathapuram, Tiruppullani and the surrounding villages, and were all accommodated in a rented house on Mada Street.

Apart from being successful in his profession, my father also took a lot of interest in social reform and participated in the affairs of the Indian National Congress. After the session at Surat in 1905, the Congress met in Madras in 1908. My father was just getting ready to go for it when my Madurai grandfather, who was staying with us, said he would also like to attend. Father tried to dissuade him: 'There was a lot of commotion in the Surat session,' he said. 'They threw chairs and tables at each other. I don't know what will happen here. You don't need to take such a risk at this age.' To this my grandfather countered: 'Is it all right for you to then go? Let whatever happens to you befall me as well.' Thus, they both attended the event.

The Passing of Sir V. Bhashyam Iyengar

In those days, there were no provision stores or co-operatives in areas such as Alwarpet, Teynampet and Mylapore. To buy anything at all, from clothes to pins, you had to go to George Town. My grandmother would set off in a bullock cart or horse carriage to George Town once a month, accompanied by a clerk, to purchase household provisions. It was on one such occasion that she suffered the greatest shock of her life.

It was 16 November 1908. Lady Bhashyam Iyengar was making purchases at Ramanujam Chetty's shop. Two people rushed in to inform her that Sir V. Bhasyam Iyengar had fainted while arguing in court. Lady

Madurai Grandfather

Bhashyam Iyengar was stunned. She immediately left for the High Court. He was already somewhat weak, and his physician had advised him to rest, but he remained immersed in his profession. That day, he had appeared in connection with an important appellate case before Justice Albert White and Justice Sir Abdul Rahim. He felt faint and during a break, went back to his chambers to rest a while. While returning to the court hall, he suffered a haemorrhage and fainted near Sir T. Muthuswami Iyer's statue.

His juniors immediately carried him to his chamber. Lady Bhashyam Iyengar did not wail on seeing her husband in that condition. Like a fire extinguished by water, she wiped her streaming eyes with her saree. She had never ever appeared in the court in the absence of her husband. She was a traditional woman after all. To see this epitome of orthodoxy who looked like Goddess Mahalakshmi, standing in the midst of so many men was a shock to everyone. Many wept.

The question arose as to whether Sir V. Bhashyam Iyengar needed to be taken to hospital or home for treatment. His wife opted for the latter; a senior doctor could be asked to visit and treat him. We received the news at our North Mada Street residence at around 5 p.m. My mother, in tears, immediately left for her parents' home. When my father returned from court, the rest of us accompanied him to Lakshmi Vilas. Grandfather was lying unconscious on a cot in the central hall, breathing faintly. Grandmother was fanning him with a hand fan. He remained that way for two days and passed away on the evening of the third day. His last rites were conducted as per tradition, in the presence of friends and relatives. His bed, chair and the silver articles he used were all given away. The charities of land, cattle, houses, education, gold and clothes were all performed as prescribed.

Subsequently, I saw a complete transformation in Grandmother. She who had always been dazzlingly bejewelled now took to wearing white, covered her head, had a garland of *tulsi* (holy basil) seeds, and sported the Vaishnavite mark on her forehead. It was clear that she was preparing herself for the hereafter. Grandmother passed away in the month of Thai (January/February) in 1926. She had made all preparations for her funerary rites, so her children were not put to any trouble. The portrait of Lord Rama that she worshipped together with the puja articles she used were all taken in a procession with pipes and drums to the Mylapore Srinivasa Perumal Temple and deposited there.

Among my maternal uncles, Venuswami Iyengar had been an invalid when young, so he was not well educated. After the death of Grandfather, he invested his share of the inheritance in the Automobile Motor Shop, Mount Road. Venu Mama married Rukmini, the fifth daughter of Kodiyalam Vasudeva Iyengar[60], during Grandfather's lifetime. They had three sons and two daughters.

---

[60] A very prominent landowner of the Kumbakonam area.

5

Vande Mataram

MY FATHER COUNTED V. KRISHNASWAMI IYER[61], DR SIR S. Mani Iyer[62] and Mylapore Gopalaswami Mudaliar[63] among his close friends. He respected these men who were his seniors in the legal profession, and often sought their advice. In his early days in law, my father, who was a junior to his father-in-law Sir V. Bhashyam Iyengar, had some misunderstanding with him and chose to apprentice himself under V. Krishnaswami Iyer. Sir S. Sankaran Nair[64] too was very close to my father. He ran a monthly titled *Social Reform* in which several prominent people,

---

[61] Right through the autobiography, Ambujammal prefixes V. Krishnaswami Iyer's name with Sir indicating that he was knighted. This is not true. He received a CIE in 1911, just before his death.

[62] Sir S. Subramania Iyer, one of the earliest Indians to become a judge of the Madras High Court, was an ardent Theosophist and a nationalist.

[63] A leading lawyer and Congressman.

[64] Sir C. (not S.) Sankaran Nair was a leading lawyer of Madras, President of the Congress in 1897, and later, a judge of the Madras High Court. He became a member of the Viceroy's Executive Council, a position he quit following the Jallianwala Bagh Massacre.

including my father, wrote articles attacking outmoded Brahminic practices and rituals that existed then. He wrote condemning child marriage and advocated post-puberty weddings. In those days, people considered people who expressed such views to be harbingers of social change and labelled them 'progressives'.

At the same time, my father began involving himself in politics. He greatly interested himself in the meetings of the Congress. This caused a lot of unease in my mother and other relatives. The Viceroy partitioned Bengal in 1905[65], and this caused the people of that province to rise in protest. Nationalists, too, expressed their opposition to this divide. But the British government paid no heed. Consequently, extremists began to make their presence felt, not just in Bengal but all over India. The seeds of national fervour had been sown in the minds of the people. Propaganda meetings and intense consultations began to take place on the ways and means to rid Mother India of her shackles. Cries of *Vande Mataram*[66] began to be heard all over India. The government was angered and ordered that those who uttered those words be imprisoned.

It was at this time that Ashe, the collector of Madurai, was killed by the revolutionary Vanchinathan[67]. The

---

[65] Announced by Lord Curzon, the Viceroy in 1905, it was rescinded six years later.

[66] 'Mother, I Bow to Thee'—the opening lines of a song in the Bengali work *Ananda Math* by Bankim Chandra Chatterjee.

[67] Robert William d'Escourt Ashe was Collector and District Magistrate

assassination resulted in the tightening of controls over South India. In particular, the police clamped down hard on Madurai District. But the extremists were not deterred and continued their activities undercover. There was apprehension that the violent tactics of the revolutionaries would permeate the Congress. Nationalistic fervour and love for the motherland spurred these activists, so the people sympathized with them. In such a situation, was it not understandable that we were afraid when our father got involved in politics?

In those days, everyone, young or old, was terrified of the police. If there was a commotion on the streets, we imagined that extremists were being chased by the police. What would happen if our father also became a revolutionary? My mother was obsessed with the fear that he would be shot dead by the police. In those days, very few people had the ability to understand the political environment, or matters of the world in general. Periodicals in Indian languages were very few, and hardly anybody had the habit of reading them. Even those from affluent families lived without bothering to know what was happening in the outside world. Women were mostly ignorant of public affairs.

After the death of my grandfather, my father did not like living in the North Mada Street house, considering it beneath his status. He decided to buy a bungalow of his

---

of Tirunelveli, and not Madurai. He was shot at point-blank range by Vanchinathan in June 1911 at Maniyachi Railway Junction.

own. Meanwhile, Lady Bhashyam Iyengar kept sending for my mother and asking her something. Elderly ladies who came home to call on my mother too had the same question. 'When are you going to conduct Ambujavalli's wedding? Has she still not reached marriageable age?' They pointed out that girls who were of my age, and that included cousin Kappu, were already married. I, to compound matters, was physically well-developed and looked older than I actually was.

Each night, there were heated discussions in hushed whispers between my parents. I conjectured that it was about my marriage prospects. They never discussed the matter in my presence. My father remained adamant for over a year that he would get me married only after I attained puberty. But the entreaties of my mother and the stern resolve of my grandmother eventually made him change his mind!

It was the practice in our household to purchase all culinary provisions once every year. These would be directly obtained from the best sources—*toor dal* for instance came from Tirupattur, *urad dal* from Madurai, and tamarind from Bangalore. Getting the toor dal to sprout, splitting the urad dal, making pickles and fritters would take over a month in summer. My mother trained me very well in all this. I was made responsible for the kitchen stores and supervising the daily doling-out of provisions.

My mother trained me in cooking as well. She purchased a new set of vessels for this and remained by my side while I learnt. Kappu also trained along with me. A desire to cook overcame me as soon as I saw those lovely vessels. The two of us vied with one another in churning out different dishes. We served our preparations to my brother on his return from school at 1.00 p.m. and anxiously awaited his verdict. He would criticize everything. We would then taste the dishes and realize he was fooling us. On the contrary, our maid, who was also served these dishes, was full of praise: 'Why do we need a cook?' she would exclaim. 'Our Pappamma's cooking is so tasty.' That delighted me.

Every evening, a devout person would come home to teach me Tamil religious poetry such as the *Thiruppavai* and the *Thirupalliezhucchi*[68]. The worship of sacred salagramas was a daily affair in our house. I was made responsible for cleaning the puja platform, drawing *kolam*[69], plucking flowers and lighting the lamps.

As I was physically well-developed by the time I was 10, I began wearing half-sarees over my skirts. These days, girls are permitted by their parents to wear half-sarees even after they reach the age of 20, so that they might seem younger than they really are. I cannot say there is anything wrong with the practice. I think our minds are shaped by the garments we wear. If I were to wear a half-saree, I would transform into a 10-year-old and be

---

[68] A set of 10 verses composed by the eighth-century poet and devotee, Tondaradipodi Alwar.
[69] Traditional patterns drawn with dry or wet rice flour at the threshold of the house or the site of worship.

playful and not bashful. On the other hand, if I were to wear a saree and have my hair plaited, I would feel I was a young maiden. Girls then become shy, and more importantly, begin living in a world of fantasy.

My mother purchased half-sarees in Dharmavaram silk for me and avoided the heavy Bangalore silks. The shops had silks from Kanchipuram, Arni, Bangalore and Dharmavaram, while a variety of cotton textiles came from Madurai. Silk sarees usually ranged between Rs 25 and Rs 30. Unlike today, we did not have much variety in sarees. Neither did customers buy in large numbers and store them. No matter how wealthy the household, the elders would buy clothes in very limited numbers for the women. New clothes were gifted on four occasions—Deepavali[70], Karthikai[71], Pongal[72] and Tamil New Year's Day[73]. These new clothes would be worn once and then be folded away, to be used on special occasions. It was back to our usual daily wear otherwise.

During the Karthikai Festival, I would wear a new half-saree and light the lamps. The oil would invariably stain the dress, and my mother would get angry, driving me to tears. My father would intervene at once and get another half-saree for me!

---

[70] The traditional festival of lights celebrated all over India in October/November.
[71] A festival of lights unique to Tamil Nadu, celebrated in November/December.
[72] The harvest festival celebrated in January, coinciding with Makar Sankranti in the rest of India.
[73] Observed in mid-April.

My mother did not often wear grand sarees or much jewellery. But she delighted in dressing me up in lace-bordered sarees and plenty of jewellery. She would even drape the nine-yard saree on me. I found it very difficult to walk in it. My mother had readied diamond ear studs, earrings, gem-encrusted necklaces, a waistband, and hairpieces for me. She had also gifted me a gold necklace of coin-shaped pendants. I also had a ruby choker. If I did not wear these on festive occasions, my mother would get upset.

A New Bungalow, and a New Life

I loved reading novels and was usually found on a sofa or a chair, reading the works of Rao Bahadur P. Sambanda Mudaliar[74], and similar authors. If my mother caught me at this, she would become angry and confiscate the books. I then took to reading them surreptitiously. I read and re-read works such as *Lovers' Eyes* several times. It would be no exaggeration to say that as a consequence, I began living in a world of make-believe. Another book I liked was the *Life History of King Bhoja*. The cover had the picture of a beautiful woman at whose feet lay Bhoja. On seeing it, I too desired to wear the same kind of half-saree that the woman was wearing. I pestered my

---

[74]Rao Bahadur Pammal Sambanda Mudaliar (1873–1964) was a pioneer of the Tamil theatre movement. He was also a prolific writer. Besides, he was a lawyer and served as a judge of the Small Causes Court.

mother to get me a half-saree with a tamarind seed pattern on it. I believed if I wore it, I too would have a prince at my feet! I must add here that one of the reasons for my living in a fantasy world was the frequent conversations among my parents and other elders about my marriage.

In that phase of life, it is natural for a young girl to resent any advice from parents, restrictions on her freedom, and being told to serve elders. I too was adamant, lazy and short-tempered. Perhaps to overcome these traits, I was pressed into many household duties by the elders. I, however, got very angry, interpreting all these tasks as various instruments of torture. It is part of ancient Indian tradition for grandmothers and aunts to keep reiterating to girls from childhood the trope of the evil mother-in-law. My mother, however, was not like that. She, on the contrary, advised me on how to behave in my wedded home—listen to the elders there, avoid laziness, perform all household chores, eschew gossip, and serve those who fell ill. In those days, such advice was always for girls, nobody paid much attention to instilling good values in boys. Discipline and good behaviour, obedience and conformance to rules were all expected of girls alone. I cannot say I paid much heed then to what my mother said. But her words were not wasted. I realize that the seeds she sowed in my mind did sprout, grow, and continued to bear fruit well into my old age.

In 1910, having searched high and low, my father purchased an old bungalow called Amjad Bagh on Luz Church Road for Rs 20,000. Before buying it, he took my mother, brother and me and showed us the place. A huge weed-infested garden that looked more like a forest went with the house. It had plenty of rain trees and monkey pod trees. The front part had *jamun*, rosary pea, wood apple and Bengal quince trees, and a banyan in the corner, apart from a couple of ponds. There was a sandalwood tree and plenty of bamboo clumps. There was no compound wall. Lantana bushes intertwined with monkey pod trees formed the boundary to the property. The house in itself was more a palace—it had a veranda running all around it, and the rooms were enormous. An aged gardener showed us around and presented us with roses from the bushes to which he tended.

On returning home, Father asked us if we liked the house. We, as children, were unanimous—we declared that we liked it immensely and asked him to buy it at once. But Mother was not so enthusiastic—she considered the house dilapidated. Moreover, the cookhouse was in a separate block, at a considerable distance from the main house. But my father would not give in. He convinced her to agree by offering to build a kitchen within the house itself. It was always like this. Father would ask Mother's opinion, but his will eventually prevailed. Mother always gave in to Father's wishes. Amjad Bagh was purchased, the old kitchen block became the cowshed, and a new one came up within the house.

That year, Mother purchased more lentils than was usual. In addition, two cooks were hired to make fritters and pappadums in enormous quantities. The rolling out of the pappadums was done by my mother and her friends, who came in large numbers to the house every afternoon. They got me to help as well. This activity went on for over a month. I could not fathom the reason for all of this. Then one day, one of mother's friends remarked that it was so sweet to see me roll out pappadums for my wedding. This was how I came to know that my marriage had been finalized!

One day, my parents called me and said they had identified a suitable match for me. The groom was academically very bright and studying for the BA degree. 'Do you want to see him for yourself?' they asked. Had I been younger, I would have responded differently. I was told that when young, I would declare that I did not want to get married and would instead prefer qualifying as a doctor. If pressed for an answer, I would say that if the groom was well qualified, I would agree. But now I was 12. The child Ambujavalli of the earlier years had morphed into a different person. When asked thus by my parents, I bashfully replied that if they had seen the groom, it was enough. They too must have thought I was a child and, therefore, incapable of a considered reply. They were satisfied with my response and proceeded with the preparations for the wedding.

I came to know that the bridegroom was studying at Presidency College and had three brothers. The family was from Kumbakonam[75] and had agricultural lands near

---

[75] A prominent town of Tamil Nadu, and located on the Cauvery River,

Valangaiman[76]. My father had declared that he would offer no dowry for his daughter. Many of his friends such as V.C. Seshachariar had agreed to this stipulation and literally beseeched my father to get me married off to one of their sons. But my mother had not agreed. My parents were not so interested in the wealth of the bridegroom's family as they were in his looks, academics, nature, and above all, his willingness to move in with us after the wedding. This Kumbakonam boy fulfilled all their expectations.

Two houses were hired—one for relatives and the other for outstation friends. With formal rituals, three processions and other ceremonies, the wedding was celebrated over five days at Amjad Bagh. While the main procession involved the bridal couple being taken around the neighbourhood, a smaller one preceding this was customary those days. This involved the bride being dressed in male attire and taken around to the place where the prospective in-laws were staying. Another girl would be decked up as the bride. This was known as 'Amman Kolam'. The intention was that the bridegroom and his parents ought to be taken in by this sudden switch. I was, therefore, dressed in a velvet suit and cap. Everyone around remarked that I looked just like my father! I was taken to the bridegroom's place, and there I

---

it is known for its temples and considered the education capital of the Madras Presidency.

[76]A village just ten kilometres from Kumbakonam, and located in the fertile Cauvery delta.

saw my prospective husband for the first time. His name was Desikachari. The wedding was celebrated in a grand fashion, and everyone praised my father for the manner in which it was conducted.

After the wedding, we shifted back to the old North Mada Street house as the kitchen was still incomplete at Amjad Bagh. My husband was asked to leave his hostel and stay with us. My father gave him a room in the front of the house. Though we lived on the same premises, as per the customs of those days, we never met or spoke to each other.

The kitchen at Amjad Bagh, when completed in 1911, was a small bungalow by itself. My father spent Rs 20,000 transforming the main house as well. Once the work was done, we shifted back into Amjad Bagh. Several rooms had come up on a foundation of granite and cement; but somehow the house lacked modernity. The first hall in it was a formal drawing room, after which came a ladies' room. A large room nearby was my father's office. The first floor had a large hall and two bedrooms. In the initial days of shifting in, we found living here to be a daunting prospect. There was hardly any footfall or vehicular traffic on the road. The Bheemannapettai[77] and Co-Operative Bank[78] areas of today were all banana plantations. The

---

[77]Now Bheemanna Mudali Street and located in Alwarpet postal district.
[78]Once the residence of Sir V.C. Desikachari, parts of it are now Sir V.C. Desika and Lady Desika roads, after a Tamil Nadu Government order banned caste suffixes from street names. The Tamil Nadu Apex

Norton Bungalow[79] was in the neighbouring D'Silva Road. To the rear of Amjad Bagh was a large bungalow named Hermitage[80]. To the west was (Sir V.C.) Desikachariar's bungalow, and opposite us was the residence of Ramachandra Rao Saheb[81] and the garden of Srinivasa Iyer. Closer to Luz were the residences of Sir K. Srinivasa Iyengar[82] and Baroda Srinivasa Iyengar[83]. On the east was Sir T. Madhav Rao's bungalow, and in Luz, next to Mylapore Club was the residence of Sundaram Iyer, and a tank named the Aratha Kuttai. That is today's Nageswara Rao Pantulu Park. Opposite the club was Lakshmi Vilas and the bungalows of Buchi Babu and V. Krishnaswami Iyer. All these houses were situated in the midst of vast gardens, so the atmosphere was always quiet.

Many changes came into our lives after we shifted into Amjad Bagh. We experienced the comforts of electricity

---

Co-Operative Bank, of which Sir Desikachariar was a founder, still occupies a part of the land.

[79]A large bungalow named after Eardley Norton, a prominent British barrister.

[80]Not a trace of this bungalow remains. It was once the residence of the Chief Secretary, Government of Madras, and later functioned as a film studio as well.

[81]Dewan Bahadur T. Ramachandra Row Saheb (1845–1906) was a legal luminary. The bungalow was called Chandra Vilas.

[82]Sir K. Srinivasa Iyengar (d. 1923) was a prominent vakil who later became a judge, Member of the Governor's Executive Council, and also Vice Chancellor, University of Madras.

[83]Dewan Bahadur S. Srinivasaraghava Iyengar (1849–1903) was a distinguished civil servant who also served as dewan (prime minister) of Baroda State from 1896 to 1901.

and a motor car for the first time. My father initially had a Wolseley and later a Napier car. A Muslim driver named Ibrahim worked for us for decades. Is it enough to purchase a large bungalow? Was it not necessary to maintain it as well? Therefore, an aged gardener to tend to the vast compound and a couple of maid servants to clean the interiors were hired. In addition, we now had a man of all work, a cowherd, an old woman, a security guard and two cooks. One of the last named always stayed at home while the other, Kasturi, accompanied my father on his travels. Raghavachari was the lawyer's clerk while Ramachandran was the typist.

Not a day went by without a rat snake or a krait or a cobra emerging from the weeds. The gardener would club them to death. During the rains, the three ponds in the middle of the banana plantations would fill up with frogs that kept up a chorus of croaks right through the night. At around midnight, jackals would begin baying.

Bheemanna Pettai and Luz Church roads being lonely thoroughfares, any woman who stepped out by herself was bound to lose her jewellery and cash. On hearing their screams, we would rush out of the bungalow, but the miscreants would have vanished. Every morning, when elderly women would come to collect the fallen banyan, jackfruit and peepal leaves, their belongings would meet with the same fate. Skirmishes between those dwelling in the hutments of Bheemanna Pettai and those in Mandaveli were matters of routine. Quite often, armed groups from one would chase those of the other right up to Luz Church Road.

Seasons when cholera and smallpox epidemics flared up filled us with fear. At least three to four biers made their way each day along Bheemanna Pettai, to the cries of 'Govinda! Govinda!' There were no vaccinations then for cholera, typhoid and other such diseases. Therefore, when these hit the surrounding localities, we did not allow our servants to go home. We took good care of them. All of us drank boiled water. In those days, the fatalities among those stricken with such diseases were very high, so people lived in mortal dread of these epidemics. During the rainy season, plague occurred frequently in Bangalore. Panic would grip the people of Madras when they heard of this. Chaos resulted when a dead rat was found anywhere in the house. The government issued orders banning travel to Bangalore and Mysore—this was the only disease-control measure they knew.

Fear gripped the educated and affluent people more than it did the poor. The latter, given the risks they faced on a daily basis, were not all that bothered. The former, on the other hand, conjured up frightening images of the diseases and adopted extreme safety measures. One year, the cry of 'Govinda!' was heard from D'Silva Road during the month of Adi (July/August). I was pregnant then. Just that morning, a visitor informed my father in a loud voice: 'Srinivasa Iyengar! Have you not heard the news? Cholera is spreading in Bheemanna Pettai, and every day there are at least 10 to 12 deaths. The people in your house need to be careful.' On hearing this, I was panic-stricken. I had taken a laxative that morning and had passed motion five or six times. I imagined this was a symptom of cholera. My parents too feared the worst. I passed the night in absolute terror. A pall of gloom hung over the house until we got to know that I was not afflicted with cholera. The power of the mind is truly amazing—it makes even the imaginary appear real.

In connection with this, I am reminded of an incident from my childhood. I had gone to Coonoor with my parents. One evening, my brother and I set out via the Bandi Shola Road to Sims Park[84]. On the way back, he suddenly said, 'Sister, I can smell the scat of a tiger. I think the animal is hiding somewhere near.' I said we needed to return home immediately and we rushed back. It was dark by the time we reached home. Mother was seated by the fireside, and we joined her there in absolute silence.

Just then, my father and a doctor friend of his walked in. The latter then said, 'Last evening, a leopard took away a dog from an Englishwoman's residence near Sims Park. You need to make sure your children don't wander far away from home during the evenings.' My brother and I were terrified on hearing this. We began to shiver, thinking of what might have been. The doctor noticed this and asked if we were feeling cold. Where was the question of

---

[84] The botanical retreat of that town was founded in 1874, and named after James Sim, Secretary to Government of Madras.

feeling cold when we were by a fire? We then narrated our going to Sims Park and rushing back. The doctor laughed. 'You were intelligent enough to come home before dark. So why are you shivering now?' he asked.

While we lived at North Mada Street, my father had a horse carriage to take him to court. Even after we purchased a car, we retained the horse carriage. It was used to take us to the beach, and my mother for her outings. Unlike today, car repair facilities were not so widespread. We, therefore, had a chauffeur who knew the technical aspects of the vehicle. In addition, we employed a cleaner who assisted the chauffeur. We also used the car sparingly.

We had so many interesting experiences shortly after buying the car. Some of these were truly terrifying. We were always on our alert when we went around in it. In the immediate aftermath of the purchase, we went on holidays to places such as Mamallapuram[85] and Tirukalukundram[86]. Even these short-distance journeys felt like long trips. We packed food and two tins of petrol for these journeys. However, we would not go beyond 20 miles! Cars were a novelty and frightening, not just to children but to adults as well. Villagers ran helter-skelter on seeing the car approaching as though they had seen the God of Death. Bullocks ran amok and despite the best efforts of the cart drivers, they sometimes dragged

---

[85] A Pallava-era port town full of rock-cut temples and bas-reliefs.
[86] An ancient temple to the south of Chennai, associated for long with two vultures appearing at midday.

their vehicles into ditches.

Once, we were going around the Ooty Race Course in our Napier car. When the vehicle reached a place occupied by Todas[87], a bison began to chase us. Our driver was quite frightened to see what looked like a young elephant. It had the strength to toss the vehicle aside. Ibrahim was a very skilled driver; he gathered speed and negotiated the curves carefully. But no matter what he did, the bison continued chasing us. Just when it appeared that the animal had gained on us, the road divided into two. Our car went uphill while the bison, with its head down, charged downhill. We could see it from our car for quite a while even as we raced home.

My father scaled great heights in his profession and, at the same time, was active in various organizations dedicated to social upliftment. He had thus earned the respect of people and the government. Once a year, the governor's wife hosted a party exclusively for women. Women from the houses of Sir V. Bhashyam Iyengar, V. Krishnaswami Iyer, P.R. Sundara Iyer, and other residents of Luz Church Road were among the invitees. I too would attend along with my mother. The preparations began at 3.00 p.m. on the day of the event. In my desire to lighten my complexion, I would wash it with soap at least three to four times. We did not then have the lotions, powders and creams we do today.

My mother would help me pleat and wear the eight-

---

[87]The indigenous community of the Nilgiri Hills.

yard Benares silk saree. I then adorned myself with a gem-studded waistband, arm band, shoulder ornaments, several bangles, necklaces, my ruby choker, ear studs and earrings, parrot-shaped brooches and nose rings. I however never wore the *bullaq*—the pendant nose ornament. My mother would then fix gold and gem-studded pieces to my hair, plait it and place flowers on the braid. She, however, contented herself with just a couple of jewellery pieces. In those days, women did not wear slippers. But we would ape the English and wear shoes and socks for this event. We journeyed either in Grandmother's chariot or our horse carriage, and reached the venue at 4.30 p.m. sharp. The governor and his wife had two official residences in the city between which they alternated—the Government House[88] on Mount Road and the Lodge[89] at Guindy. State events took place at the Banqueting Hall[90] on Mount Road.

At 4.30 p.m., the governor's wife began receiving visitors at the top of the stairs by shaking hands with each person as they came in. Music would be heard from inside the hall and women conversed in groups. Snacks and ice cream were served. We returned home at 6.00 p.m. In our thinking, a visit to the governor's house was akin to a journey to heaven.

There would be intense discussions among us women on the First Lady's looks, her clothes and jewellery. High-

---
[88] Later known as Admiralty House, it was demolished in 2010.
[89] The present Raj Bhavan.
[90] Renamed Rajaji Hall and inside the Omandurar Government Estate.

society ladies of Madras were known to spin tall tales. One of these concerned a governor's wife who each year sojourned in England for six months and returned looking at least 20 years younger. It was said that she had her face enamelled every time she went home to England!

The governor went about in a carriage drawn by six horses, and on such occasions had a bodyguard cavalry accompanying him. He stayed in Madras only for six months—during the cooler part of the year. During summer, he moved to Ootacamund and the entire government shifted with him, functioning from a place called Stone Hill there. Accommodation was provided there for all government functionaries.

In those days, people considered Englishmen and Englishwomen as belonging to a superior class. Why, even the Brahmin priests spoke of them as celestials! But there never was a desire among Indians to ape Westerners in matters of dress or ostentatious living. Once, a high-placed Indian in Madras had gone with his wife to attend an official event. There, when the governor extended his hand in greeting to the lady, she did not take it but folded hers in a namaste. This was written about in the newspapers of the day as an insult to the governor. The governor held an annual event known as the levee at his residence. It was considered mandatory for senior government officials, high court judges and leaders of society to attend it. At this event, the gubernatorial couple would stand at one end of the Banqueting Hall. Those who attended lined up in strict order of precedence, and shook hands with the governor. They then went down on one knee, took the hand of the governor's wife, pressed it to their lips and walked backward to their seats.

Dinner invites too came from the governor's residence. As alcohol was served and the menu was largely non-vegetarian at these events, the orthodox in Madras hesitated to attend. If they did not, it was considered an insult. Many attended and came away without eating or drinking anything. My father was one such person. Of course, there were others who ate everything on the sly and came back home claiming they had touched nothing.

My mother read English novels and could speak the language passably well. Given the irregular nature of my education, it became necessary to tutor me in spoken English, so I could converse freely at the governor's events. Miss Violet, an Anglo-Indian, was employed for this. She came home every day for an hour and taught me to speak and write in English.

Journeys to Kodaikanal

We began going to Kodaikanal instead of Ootacamund every summer. Going there meant getting off the train at Ammaiyanayakanur, also known as Kodaikanal Road Station, and proceeding to Periyakulam in a covered cart pulled by two bullocks. From there, we were taken in *doli*s or palanquins to Kodaikanal. If we left by bullock cart at 11.00 a.m., we reached Periyakulam by 7.00 p.m. My father sent a cook to Kodaikanal Road a day before we left Madras. He awaited us with coffee and breakfast when we reached there. We bathed at the station, had our food, and then boarded the bullock cart. Hay was spread in layers inside the cart and covered with our rugs and mattresses. We sat on these comfortably and proceeded onwards. My parents, brother and I would be in one cart and the cook with the luggage in another. A fresh pair of oxen was arranged for every 10 miles at villages such as Vattalagundu and Devadanapatti.

The night was spent in Periyakulam, at the residence of a lawyer friend of my father's. The next morning, we left at around 6.00 a.m. by bullock cart and reached the foothills. There, by the Silver Cascade waterfall, we prepared *upma* and coffee on a stove and boarded the waiting palanquins bound for Kodaikanal. My father and K.V. Krishnaswami Iyer[91] purchased two adjoining bungalows there. Ours was named Lidcote[92]. Not many Indians went to Kodaikanal those days; it was preferred by Europeans. The place did not have many shops. A weekly shandy (local market) was where we purchased all our requirements. My mother packed and brought in tins from Madras carrying all the provisions we needed

---

[91]Rao Saheb K.V. Krishnaswami Iyer (1885–1965) was a prominent lawyer who was better known for championing public causes. He was founder of the Madras Library Association, and the second and longest-serving President of the Music Academy, Madras. He and Ambujammal's father were neighbours on North Mada Street.

[92]It was customary for most houses in hill stations to be named after villages and places in England. Lidcote took its name from a village in Buckinghamshire.

for a month. A cook, a maid and a man of all work accompanied us. We also brought blankets, woollen clothes, socks, etc., with us. Despite all this, we found it unbearably cold, and at night, I would tie a pillow on my back to warm myself.

My father's friend K. Ayyavayyar came to Kodaikanal each summer. He had two daughters who went around the place without wearing any warm clothing, much to my envy. 'Why don't they catch a cold?' I wondered. My father went walking every evening and returned by 8.00 p.m. Sixty years ago, there was no electricity in Kodaikanal. The houses were lit by kerosene lamps and candles, and as for the streets, they were pitch dark. There was a huge lake in which boating was a popular recreation. We could watch this from a boat club. Friends and acquaintances were invariably met around the lake area. There were occasions when the day of the annual rites for ancestors came about while we were in Kodaikanal. In order to ensure there was no break in the observance, my father ensured Brahmins came from Madurai and performed the rites in all solemnity.

Once, when my grandfather Bhashyam Iyengar was holidaying in Ootacamund, he had to perform the annual rite for his ancestors. He had 10 Brahmins brought from Madras for this. As feeding crows was essential during this rite, and as Ootacamund had none owing to its elevation, a few of these birds were captured in Madras and brought in cages!

I Attain Puberty

When I was 13, I attained puberty and as per tradition, I was taken in procession on the fourth day to the pond in Lakshmi Vilas and ceremonially bathed. My mother wanted news of my coming-of-age to be sent by a messenger, accompanied with appropriate gifts, to my in-laws in Kumbakonam. My father, however, did not agree; he merely sent a letter. This enraged my in-laws no end. My mother also wanted me, after the purificatory bath, to be seated in a decorated pavilion where women invitees would sing. My father and I were completely against this, so the idea was given up. As I had come of age, my mother terminated my violin classes as well.

Around this time, my father began to travel increasingly as his legal practice expanded tremendously. It became rare for him to be at home even on festive occasions. In those days, his monthly income exceeded Rs 20,000! The clerk maintained the accounts, which my mother oversaw. There was a steady stream of guests in our house, and attending to them took up all my mother's and my time.

A Ladies' Club

In those days, unlike today, there were no music *sabha*s or cinema theatres in every locality. A silent film was screened occasionally at some places. Apart from festivals and weddings, women had no recreational activities.

Barrister N. Subrahmanyam[93], a Brahmin by birth, converted to Christianity. He lived at the bungalow called The Hermitage. The C.S.I. Kalyani Hospital on Edward Elliots Road was set up by him in his mother's name and gifted to the Christian Mission. His wife was a close friend of my mother's.

She, my mother, Sita Thiruvenkatachari, Lady Devadoss[94], and others began a recreation club for women at Norton Lodge. They would meet twice a week and play tennis, badminton, ring tennis and other games. Mrs Madeley[95] was secretary and Mrs Namberumal Chetty[96] was treasurer. Besides them, Miss Andrews, Mrs Hensman[97], Mrs Perth, and other Englishwomen too joined as members. The governor's wife was President ex-officio of this club. The institution grew rapidly. High-society ladies from Egmore, such as the daughters of Sir Sankaran Nair and Justice Krishnan[98], joined.

---

[93]Dewan Bahadur N. Subrahmanyan (1841–1911) was Administrator General, Government of Madras.

[94]Lady Masilamoney Chellammal Devadas, the wife of Justice Sir David Devadoss and a prominent social worker in her own right, was among the first batch of women councillors elected to the Corporation of Madras.

[95]Wife of J.W. Madeley, Engineer, Corporation of Madras, and practically the father of the Kilpauk Water Works. Madeley's Subway in T. Nagar commemorates him.

[96]Nacharamma was the wife of Dewan Bahadur T. Namberumal Chetty, the builder baron and contractor who put up most of the prominent buildings of Madras.

[97]Wife of J.M. Hensman, Health Officer of the Corporation of Madras.

[98]Justice Sir Cheruvari Krishnan (1868–1927).

I, too, was a member. Within a few days, the club took on a bungalow called Sylvan Lodge[99] in Mylaporeat at a monthly rent of Rs 50. By then, Mrs Madeley and Mrs C.S. Thiruvenkatachari were the secretaries. For a very long time, Mother was the treasurer.

On seeing us visiting the club regularly, the orthodox and elderly began saying we had taken to dancing like Englishwomen. They lamented that the club had led us to neglect our duties at home.

My father was not someone who readily permitted my mother and me to go out, but he allowed us to join the club. Outings to the club were not only recreational but also beneficial to my health. Belying the fears of the elders, not one of the women neglected their domestic duties because of club activities. On the contrary, we always ensured we had completed all our chores before we set out. We took care that our husbands or children did not suffer in any way, so no one could really fault us. In fact, we attended to all our duties with greater enthusiasm and speed than before. We went to the club by 4.30 p.m. and returned by 6.30 p.m., just before dark. We did not play cards but played games such as shuttlecock, badminton and tennis. If we felt thirsty, we drank iced water or soda. No coffee, tea or snacks were served. Due to the club, our social network widened.

Classes were started to teach English to married

---

[99] Located on D'Silva Road, this house belongs to the David Devadoss family and still survives.

women like me, whose knowledge of the language was limited. The prime mover behind this was Mrs Madeley, who despite being Irish, interested herself in the development of Indian women. She wanted Indian women to bestir, think, and express themselves freely like their Western counterparts. Miss Gunther[100], and a sister of Miss de la Haye[101], were our teachers. The classes took place between 11.00 a.m. and 3.00 p.m. at the club premises. There were two groups—senior and junior. In the former were those like Aunt Janammal, V. Krishnaswami Iyer's daughter Subbalam[102] and Agli. In the latter were those like myself, Dr Rangappa's[103] daughter Yamuna, K. Savitri Ammal[104] and Sundaram Iyer's daughter. A few months later, Mrs Sathyanathan began taking classes for us. We were now taught drawing, painting, tailoring, history, geography and maths. The English classes now included the plays of Shakespeare. The governor's wife, Lady Haringe[105], would often come

---

[100] Miss Ida Gunther of the Indian Educational Service.

[101] Miss Dorothy de la Haye was the first principal of Queen Mary's College.

[102] K. Subbulakshmi Ammal.

[103] Dr H. Rangappa of the Madras Medical College and the General Hospital.

[104] K. Savitri Ammal was an elder daughter of V. Krishnaswami Iyer.

[105] Ambujammal's memory is playing tricks here. Lord Hardinge was never Governor of Madras. But the founding of the club in 1911 was during his viceroyalty. As Lady Hardinge is unlikely to have taken interest in a club in distant Madras, Ambujammal must be referring to Lady Carmichael, wife of the then governor of Madras.

to the club. She taught the younger members to crochet, and we made lovely floral designs.

I found going to the club, interacting with other women and playing sports with them to be a novel experience. Thus far, I had led a sheltered existence, not interacting with society, not broadening my mind, remaining ignorant of world matters, and closeted within my family. This new experience led to some new thoughts arising in my mind. Looking back, I can only marvel at the way I had lived till then.

Very rarely did you see women who were highly qualified or engaged in social service. I began to wonder at how Indian women were leading the existence of proverbial frogs in the well. Even though I was young and not well-educated, owing to my marriage while still a child, I had plenty of opportunities to broaden my outlook. These days, parents view (and treat) even 20-year-old daughters as young children. The girls too think that way and behave irresponsibly. Outside of their school and college education, they lack experience and wisdom which contribute to maturity.

Though they were not well-educated, women of my era were not like this. Owing to lack of opportunities, they were unable to display their talents, rather like flames covered by smoke. Thus, in comparison to Western women, their Indian counterparts seemed backward. Despite this, history has shown that when faced with challenging circumstances, Indian women took on onerous responsibilities and showed that they possessed the necessary intellect to handle them.

Social interaction and education can be considered the keys of the mind; experience is what stokes the brain. But still, what is not ingrained cannot be given by education or experience. Our ancient culture and traditions determine our life's journey. Our nature does not come to us because of education or experience. It is the result of the good and the bad that we did in various births. As far as I was concerned, the experience I gained at the recreation club created in me a maturity that later enabled me to devote myself to social uplift.

Meanwhile, my husband had graduated in law and apprenticed himself under my father. I never went to my mother-in-law's house after my marriage. Other than the fact that he had three brothers and no sisters, I knew nothing about his family. As my husband had moved in with us after our wedding, there was no further contact with his family. I learnt that my father-in-law was offended with my parents, chiefly because no dowry had been offered and the news of my attaining puberty had not been intimated in a ceremonial fashion, as dictated by tradition. Moreover, my father's tough nature was not the kind that could build relationships with my husband's family. They were deeply upset that contrary to what was expected from the bride's parents, my father had neither kept up an active correspondence with them nor offered his respects, as and when the occasion demanded. Therefore, my in-laws never wished to see or invite me to their home.

I never met any of my in-laws after the first Deepavali after marriage. But when we received news of my mother-in-law's passing, I too got ready to go to Kumbakonam along with my husband. My father was not keen on this but gave into my entreaties. My mother sent Cheema Chitti, a grandaunt, as my companion. On reaching Kumbakonam, my husband went to his house while my grandaunt and I stayed at the residence of my aunt Kalyani in Reddiar Tank Street.

That afternoon, I was seated on the platform outside the house when an old lady came rushing in and exclaimed, 'Are you Desikan's wife? The city girl? Have you only now discovered the route to your mother-in-law's place? Did you care to visit her during the four years that she was bedridden?'

I was mortified and close to tears. My aunt immediately intervened: 'Why blame such a young girl?' she countered. 'What will she know? After all, she can visit only if they invite her. And who are you to ask this?'

The old woman took offence and left, retorting, 'All I wanted to do was explain things to an ignorant girl, and here I am being branded as evil!'

'What kind of a town is this?' I asked my aunt. 'She just came and tried to draw me into an argument without even a formal introduction! Imagine what more she would have said had I known her from before! Is Kumbakonam full of quarrelsome people?' From then on, I began to dislike and even dread people from that town.

The obsequies lasted ten days. It was the custom in my

family that when women travelled by car, horse carriage or bullock cart, there was always a chaperone and a male escort. Every morning, my grandaunt took me by bullock cart to my husband's home and brought me back to my aunt's house in the evening. When we arrived on day one, my father-in-law apparently asked as to why I had come. It is possible that he had felt that way as my first visit was for a sorrowful and not a happy occasion.

The housework was performed entirely by my sisters-in-law. There were no cooks. I appreciated the way they actively went about their duties, but I found their orthodoxy and their behaviour novel to say the least. I disliked all of it. I could not help wondering at the contrast between Amjad Bagh and this house on Iyengar Street, Kumbakonam. They could have been two different worlds!

On the tenth day, just before the offering of rice to the departed soul, all the women of the house, as per custom, rolled in the dust on the street, beat their breasts, and began to lament. An old lady asked me to do the same. But I could do nothing. They mocked me for standing like a pillar. When Grandfather died, Lady Bhashyam Iyengar had done none of this! She was the picture of dignity, weeping silently. I did not even do that. I just stood watching.

We all then went to the Cauvery for bathing. I was terrified of the river, nor had I ever bathed in the open before—I just did not know how to. Somehow, I managed to dip myself in the water with the assistance of the women around. We returned as per custom in wet clothes and that night I fell ill with influenza. Fortunately, it was a mild attack and three days later, I returned to Madras. This was my first and last visit to my in-laws' place. Having been there, I could understand the circumstances in which my husband had been brought up. I observed all my in-laws closely during the ten days I was there. From their conversations and practices, I formed my conclusions. They were of orthodox, ordinary stock and believed in outmoded customs. They were narrow-minded and considered women to be inferior to men. Though educated in the traditional sense, they were arrogant.

Even in my family there were orthodox people, such as Lady Bhashyam Iyengar and my Madurai grandfather, Seshadri Iyengar. But they never went to such extremes as these people. My family was broad-minded and always considered women equal to men. They were well-read but not arrogant.

Within a few days of our return to Madras, there was a slight difference of opinion between Father and my husband. At first, I did not grasp the reasons behind this, but later my mother explained it all. My husband had received a letter from his father stating he would not be receiving his monthly allowance from Kumbakonam henceforth, as he was married to a wealthy lawyer's daughter. He would need to look to my father for sustenance in future. Unable to talk to anyone about it, my husband was in a state of suppressed anger. My father came to know of this from his clerk and was greatly angered at my father-in-law. He berated him as a greedy man, but he did not display his displeasure to my husband. 'Why did you not feel free to talk to me about this?' he asked him.

Later, at my mother's intervention, it was decided that my husband would get a monthly allowance of Rs 100. This inconsequential argument sowed seeds of doubt in me—had my husband married me for my wealth?

For all his phenomenal earnings, my father was a frugal man. He never allowed ostentatious expenditure. His strictness and short temper made life difficult for us. My brother was terrified to even approach him. Father would lose his temper if any of us or the servants did something he did not approve of. Everyone lived in dread of his fury, and he took it out on Mother. She was answerable for everything.

Being an active man, he abhorred sloth. Even while talking, he paced up and down. He was awake at six and till 10 in the morning was busy with legal matters and discussions with clients. He then bathed quickly, had a meal, wore his legal robes, and left for the court. On his departure, a great silence would descend on the house—as though a thunderstorm had just ended. On his return, the house would resound with him discussing cases with his apprentices and chivvying the servants.

For all his legendary temper, he cooled down quickly and would shower love on us. We concluded that externally he was fiery and tough, but at heart he was a child. We had greater love and affection for our mother. Her patience, her capacity to subsume her desires to cater to ours, and her ability to adjust to my father elevated her in our estimation.

World War I

World War I began in 1914. The Kaiser, as the German Emperor was referred to, invaded France via Belgium. England and other countries came to the aid of France, so the war began. India as a British colony sent its troops to France. That year, in September, the German ship *Emden* bombarded the Madras harbour. The oil tankers at the port caught fire and burnt for three days. Consequently, residents of the city were petrified. Several left for their villages. British warships began keeping watch over the coast, but there was no bombardment thereafter. We received news about the Gurkha regiment from India fighting bravely at Flanders.

As the war went on for three to four years, we at the club began conducting fundraising events. We prepared savouries at home and sold them at specially held bazaars, the proceeds going to the war fund. Mrs Madeley also got us involved in preparing kit bags, bandages, shirts and handkerchiefs for soldiers at the front. We felt very proud of our service. The government honoured those who spearheaded such efforts by conferring the Kaiser-i-Hind medal on them; Mrs Madeley was also a recipient.

My Health

I conceived in 1914 and my health began to decline. I was taken to Dr Macphail[106], a lady doctor belonging to the Scottish Mission. She diagnosed that I was afflicted with tuberculosis and began treatment. One-and-a-half litres of milk was boiled till it was half the volume, and I was given the same to drink. I was advised to include fish and eggs in my diet. I was encouraged to walk in the open, do a spot of gardening, and sleep in the open at night. I was cured in six months.

Miss Macphail was a very talented doctor and was then working in a hospital at Kanchipuram. Every year, she would go off to the hills on a two-month furlough. Being a native of Scotland, she loved the mountains and climbing them. She invariably went to Darjeeling in the Himalayan foothills. In those days, Indian women gynaecologists were rare, and the profession had only English women. Our people hesitated to consult male doctors and deliveries were left to traditional midwives, even if the case was complicated.

I delivered a baby boy three days after the *Emden* bombardment. They named him Krishnaswami. Immediately after, I fell ill for three months. I could not breastfeed the baby and a wet nurse was employed for this. As I was weakening steadily, eminent TB specialist

---

[106]Dr Alexandrina Matilda Macphail (1860–1946) was a well-known doctor who founded the Christina Rainey Hospital in Madras.

Dr Keshav Pai[107] was called in. He diagnosed that my lungs had no TB but the disease had infected my stomach! He prescribed a special diet—no rice, and I was to have plenty of vegetables and fruits. On seeing the list of items, I realized I needed a cook exclusively for my meals. I hated the special diet. 'Give me medicines, tablets or injections. But I cannot live without eating rice—especially curd rice,' I declared. I ate just bland curd rice for two years. Gradually, the problems with my bowels, my aches and pains ceased, and I improved till I was completely cured.

My Brother's Education and His Leg

When my brother was in the ninth standard, he went to the Nilgiris. There, he had a fall and injured his hip and leg and was bedridden for a year. He was a keen student and was badly affected by this break in his studies. My father arranged for a tuition master to come home and teach my brother, even as he lay in bed. Dr Niblock[108] operated on him and affected a cure, but even after that my brother walked with a limp. Despite all this, he went to University Hall, climbed up the steps using a walking stick, wrote the exam and passed. He joined Presidency College where my father had once studied.

Illnesses of various kinds began afflicting my family at this time. My baby suffered from stomach aches and

---

[107]Rao Bahadur Dr M. Keshava Pai.
[108]Dr W.J. Niblock of the Indian Medical Service, who later became a pioneering gastroenterologist.

fevers owing to the malpractices of the wet nurse. My mother was afflicted with heart disease and was frequently bedridden. I, therefore, had to take on the responsibility of running the house and caring for the ailing. Despite all this, I made sure I regularly went to the club and attended the classes.

In 1915, my father was appointed Advocate General. That was when we purchased the Napier car. That year, my Madurai grandfather, Seshadri Iyengar, suddenly passed away. We received the news at 2.00 p.m., and my father organized a special train to take him there from Madras. My mother accompanied him. My brother and I did not go. My father was awarded the CIE for the exemplary manner in which he went about his duties as Advocate General.

Getting to Know Gandhiji

At that time, Mahatma Gandhi came from Africa to India to raise funds for the South Africa Satyagraha Movement and to garner the support of Indians. He was accorded a rousing welcome when he first came to Madras. The Gandhi couple were guests of G.A. Natesan, Editor of the *Indian Review*. My father organized a garden party for them. Several garden parties had been held on our premises. When my mother hosted one for Lady Pentland, the wife of the governor, catering was done by the well-known English hotel, Harrisons. The band played and the party was a grand success. But for the

Gandhis, the bill of fare was entirely different—boiled peanuts, coconut scrapings, apples, oranges, grapes, dates and such fruits, cashew nuts, almonds, pistachios and other such dry fruits, water, buttermilk, tender coconut water and jaggery-flavoured water!

Several prominent English people came for the event. Some had invited themselves over out of curiosity to see Gandhiji. My mother and I did not participate. Those were times when it was considered improper for women to talk to men who were not family members, to participate with them in public events, or to be seated as their equals. My mother and I, therefore, remained in the hall at the rear of the house. Once the tea party was over, my father brought Kasturba Gandhi in to introduce us to her. I was in a silk saree and wearing all my diamond jewellery. She, on the other hand, was in a simple white cotton saree draped in the Gujarati style. There were no jewels on her barring a pair of bangles, and these were not of gold or silver. They were of iron! She was like the wife of a Gujarati farmer! On seeing her effulgent eyes and the motherly love on her face, I experienced several emotions. Gandhiji was dressed in a white dhoti, the traditional Indian shirt and a turban. Everyone marvelled at the simplicity of this couple.

The next morning, my mother and I took Kasturba to our club. It was customary there for us to greet each other in Western style with 'Hello', 'Good Evening', 'Goodbye' and 'Ta Ta'. But to our surprise, she chose to respond with the traditional namaste, palms pressed together. That evening, we escorted her to the public meeting at the V.P. Hall[109]. As it was an event for men, we did not participate but waited outside in our car after showing Kasturba in. We were awed and even somewhat intimidated by the size of the crowd outside the hall.

A Raft of Troubles

Within a few days of the above event, a tragedy befell me. I can even say it transformed my life forever. For some time prior to this, my husband had been engrossed in reading certain books and practising some yogic exercises and also swimming in tanks, etc. He was also following an ascetic diet. None of us could fathom the reason for this transformation. He and my father were studies in contrast. He was an introvert who never expressed his feelings, even to me, and was, therefore, a puzzle to us. Despite living in our household, he never grew close to any of us. Nor did he seem to have any liking for his hometown or his relatives. After coming to Madras, he never ever spoke of them.

One day, he simply vanished. That evening, we got to know he was in Saidapet, at our relative's house. My father immediately sent his clerk to fetch him. My parents thought my husband had left home in a huff and began planning ways to placate him. They even thought

---

[109] The Victoria Public Hall, built in 1887 to commemorate the golden jubilee of Queen Victoria's reign and meant to be the town hall. It still stands as a prominent landmark.

there had been a quarrel between us. Considering his introverted nature, and his inability to confide in me, we had never had any opportunity to argue. Where then was the question of him leaving in a huff? He was brought home that evening in a barely sentient state. I cannot bring myself to describe our shock, even after so many years. A British doctor was immediately brought in by my father. A separate residence and servants were organized for my husband, but even after two months of treatment, there was no improvement. The doctor felt that my husband needed to be committed to an institution.

Neither my father-in-law nor my brothers-in-law ever bothered to find out what had happened. What to say of my husband's other relatives? The entire burden, therefore, fell on my father. He was quite clear that he did not wish to send his son-in-law to a mental asylum. It was, therefore, decided that my husband would be treated by the famed Malayali Ayurvedic doctor Thrissur Mooss[110]. A house was rented in Thrissur, and my husband was sent there with a cook, servant and clerk. Treatment in the Malayalam style began and went on for six years at a monthly cost of Rs 500.

My son was around one-and-a-half when this happened. My mother was so shocked at the turn my life had taken that her heart condition worsened. It was left to me to

---

[110] Eledath Thaikattu Narayanan Mooss was a renowned ashtavaidya or practitioner of the Ayurvedic system of medicine in Kerala. His son Neelakantan Mooss founded the Vaidyaratnam Oushadhashala, which still flourishes.

run the house. Given the volume of work, I had no time to brood over my fate, which in a way was a blessing. But each morning when I awoke, I would find my pillow wet with my tears. I considered tears to be the sole solace for women faced with sorrow.

The Home Rule Movement

Col. Olcott and Madame Blavatsky had together founded the Theosophical Society[111]. Annie Besant[112], an Englishwoman, was their disciple. She became President of the Theosophical Society after Olcott passed away. She respected Indian traditions and practices. At the same time, she worked hard to reform society by ridding us of superstitions and blind beliefs. She also addressed the issue of the upliftment of women and the downtrodden. She had many adherents to her way of thinking. These included V.C. Seshachariar, Dr Sir S. Subramania Iyer, Dr Srinivasamurti[113], C.P. Ramaswami Iyer, and several

---

[111] Col. H.S. Olcott, an American, and Madame Helena Blavatsky, a Russian aristocrat, together founded the Theosophical Society in 1874 in the USA. In 1879, they relocated to Adyar, Madras, and the society has remained headquartered here ever since.

[112] Annie Besant (1847–1933) was a social reformer, women's rights activist, writer, orator and an ardent Theosophist. She championed Home Rule for Ireland and India.

[113] Capt. Dr G. Srinivasamurti (1887–1962) was an Ayurvedic practitioner and a Theosophist. He became the first principal of the Government School of Indian Medicine, Kilpauk, which later made way for the Kilpauk Medical College. His statue is still on the premises.

other prominent Indians and Englishmen. The disciples sought her blessings in the Indian way—by falling at her feet—and carried forward her ideals of social reform. This was not to the liking of orthodox Hindus who were forever ready with a litany of abuse for Annie Besant and her followers.

Those were times when if a man offered his respects to a woman, it was considered uncivilized and also a subject of derision. 'No matter what good she has done, it is a matter of shame to our society that our men prostrate before her,' cried several elderly people. 'Moreover, she is a foreigner. We have fallen on bad times.'

Thus far, the Congress had merely demanded an increased role in governance for Indians but had not passed a resolution demanding independence. Doctor Besant felt India ought to be independent and began the Home Rule Movement for this. Many prominent people joined in, and there was fresh enthusiasm in fighting for freedom. Dr Besant began *New India*, a newspaper, for the cause. Meetings were held all over the country and fiery speeches were delivered. When Mrs Besant returned to Madras after a successful tour of the country, she was accorded an enthusiastic welcome with traditional honours and taken in procession down Mylapore. Unbeknown to my father, my aunt Janammal and I witnessed this. I consider this to be the first awakening of nationalistic pride in me. My aunt and I came away astounded with Mrs Besant. My father, on the other hand, detested her. He was an orthodox man and, therefore, strongly opposed the principles and practices of the Theosophical Society. His close friendship with Dr Nanjunda Rao[114], our family physician, was another reason for this dislike.

Initially a member of the society, Dr Rao disassociated himself owing to his total abhorrence of the esoteric practices followed there. He also disbelieved that Theosophists communicated directly with sages and the gods. He vented his opinions when he visited us. My father, therefore, opposed Mrs Besant's views when he spoke in public meetings. Once, he accused her of falsehoods, and there was a prolonged debate over this in the newspapers, with accusations and counters. It delighted the reading public.

As Mrs Besant's movement strengthened, clashes with the police at meetings and incidents of stone throwing began to increase. Lord Willingdon, then Governor of Madras, was keen that she be designated a revolutionary and a disturber of public peace. As per convention, he sought the views of my father, who was then Advocate General. No matter what his differences of opinion were with Dr Besant, he did not consider her Home Rule Movement illegal and expressed his views as such to the governor. The latter, however, was not willing to accept this. My father was asked to reconsider.

---

[114]Dr M.C. Nanjunda Rao (1862–1921), a prominent medical practitioner of Mylapore, was also an ardent follower of Swami Vivekananda. Nanjunda Rao Colony in Mylapore commemorates him.

'Mrs Besant is a leader who commands the respect and love of thousands. Moreover, she is an Englishwoman. She cannot, therefore, be arrested like others. It is best she is taken to a hill station and confined to house arrest,' was my father's recommendation. Acting as per this, Mrs Besant was detained in a bungalow in Ootacamund.

The Rowlatt Act

At the end of World War I, the British promulgated the Rowlatt[115] Act ostensibly to bring in reforms to the way India was governed. Many leaders including Mahatma Gandhi had believed that Indians would get more rights, owing to their wholehearted participation in the war effort. But to their disappointment, the Act gave them nothing. People rose in protest and the Jallianwala Bagh massacre[116] was a direct result of this.

Following that incident, Gandhiji began the Civil Disobedience Movement. He also planned to collect Rs 1 crore for the Tilak Swarajya Fund. My aunt Janammal and I participated in the fundraising effort. I was then

---

[115] The Anarchical and Revolutionary Crimes Act 1919 was named after Sir Sidney Rowlatt, Bar-at-Law who headed the committee that formulated it. As per this, the government could keep suspected revolutionaries indefinitely in prison, without trial.

[116] Often considered the beginning of the end of the British Raj, this incident took place on 13 April 1919 in an enclosed garden in Amritsar when, as per the instructions of Brig. R.E.H. Dyer, Gurkha troops fired on people who had gathered to protest against the arrest of some freedom fighters. Several died and many more were injured.

learning Sanskrit in the evenings at her house. On the eighteenth of each month, observed as Tilak Day, we fasted and collected funds.

The Civil Disobedience Movement began in the North and slowly gained ground throughout the country, following Gandhiji's call to the people. In particular, he appealed to lawyers and government servants to give up their professions and join the movement.

Those were days when I had plenty of opportunity to read the newspapers and periodicals that carried Gandhiji's speeches and reports about the movement he had begun. I read his book *Key to Health* several times over, and the principles he expounded in it became firmly ingrained in me. Gandhiji often spoke of rebirth. I felt I had had one following my reading of his book. I embarked on a new path. He had written that husband and wife ought to change to living like siblings in the service of the nation, and I felt that this was particularly appropriate for me. I adopted Gandhiji as my preceptor.

Involvement with the Congress

My father, who initially considered the Civil Disobedience Movement to be against the law, changed his mind following the Jallianwala Bagh massacre. He resigned from his position as Advocate General and renounced his CIE. The provincial leadership of the Congress met in Tirunelveli in 1921, and my father was invited to preside. Having done so, he returned to Madras and became a committed Congress activist. His speech at Tirunelveli captivated the people, and several came forward to join the nationalist cause. Our whole family became followers of Gandhiji.

We collected all foreign garments we had at home and these were consigned to flames by Father at the seashore, in the middle of a massive meeting. This marked the formal beginning in Madras of the boycott of foreign goods. From then on, we as a family wore only hand-spun khadi. Our diamonds were all locked up in the iron safe. My mother and I began wearing simple jewels of pearls set in gold. The portraits that adorned our drawing room were replaced with those of Tilak[117], Lala Lajpat Rai[118], C.R. Das[119], Motilal Nehru[120], Gopalkrishna Gokhale[121], Mahatma Gandhi, S. Subramania Iyer, and other patriots.

It was during Gandhiji's Civil Disobedience Movement that there occurred many changes to my life.

---

[117] Lokmanya Bal Gandgadhar Tilak (1856–1920) was in many ways Mahatma Gandhi's predecessor in the freedom movement.

[118] Punjab Kesari Lala Lajpat Rai (1865–1928) was an author, a freedom fighter and an insurance pioneer.

[119] Deshbandhu Chittaranjan Das (1870–1925) was a leading lawyer and patriot from Bengal.

[120] Motilal Nehru (1861–1931) was the leader of the Allahabad Bar and later a freedom fighter. His son was Pandit Jawaharlal Nehru.

[121] Gopal Krishna Gokhale (1866–1915) was the founder of the Servants of India Society and a moderate in the freedom struggle.

Life Takes a New Direction

My devotion to Gandhiji led me to learn to become aware of our spiritual tenets. I began reading Swami Vivekananda's *Bhakti Yoga*, the Tamil translation of Lokamanya Bal Gangadhar Tilak's *Gita Rahasya*, called *Gitasaram*, and other works on Indian spirituality. My mind rejected the exclusive pursuit of knowledge or devotion. I felt service which combined duty, knowledge and devotion was the best. I began taking steps along that route.

Having read Sri Chandavarkar's[122] book, I decided to speak only the truth and even practised this for a week. I cannot enumerate the challenges I faced during those seven days! Gandhiji had written that he had decided to speak the truth only after watching the Harishchandra play[123]. I, too, decided to follow his example. Even though I cannot say I met with complete success in this endeavour, I found I could not utter falsehoods with the same impunity as I did earlier.

My mind gradually began to transform.

I was the typical rich man's daughter. I had till then

---

[122]Sir Narayan Ganesh Chandavarkar (1855–1923) was a Hindu reformer, Vice Chancellor of the University of Bombay and President of the Indian National Congress.

[123]Satyawadi Raja Harishchandra was a mythical king who spoke only the truth and faced several travails as a consequence, before eventually triumphing. Mahatma Gandhi has made several references to the impact the former's life story had on him.

lived with no concern for the nation or for others—I was arrogant and selfish. Thus far, I had believed that devotion and worship of gods were rules laid down by the elders for our personal well-being alone. But now, I began to realize that attaining an unworldly goal was the sole purpose of devotion.

Ever since my husband had become incurably ill, all my dreams had been shattered. I had no support from his side of the family. I was fated to lead my entire life as a dependent of my parents. I have earlier written about how based on my father's opinion as Advocate General, Mrs Besant had been interred in Ootacamund. In my ignorance, I had even felt that my domestic troubles were divine retribution for this sin.

In the midst of all this, we were informed that my father-in-law had passed away in Kumbakonam. This time, I did not accompany my husband. That was his last visit to his birthplace. Despite all the treatment he had received, it could not be said that my husband was completely cured. He had to be sent to Thrissur every year for a couple of months for treatment, failing which he began displaying symptoms of insomnia and mental disturbances. Due to his illness, he became a transformed individual. Till then, a Western-educated modern man, he had morphed into an orthodox Brahmin. He was forever immersed in the Puranas or in rituals, and shunned human contact. He lost interest in all worldly matters and became a loner. Following his return from Kumbakonam after the obsequies for his father, he lost all contact with his relatives. He was also unable to continue with his legal practice.

The wedding of my brother to Soundaram, the only daughter of Poondi Seshadri Iyengar, then Principal of Benaras Hindu University, was conducted in a very grand fashion at Tirucchanur. My brother Parthasarathy completed his law degree and apprenticed himself under, and later became junior to, S. Doraiswami Iyer[124], one of the prominent lawyers of Madras. Doraiswami Iyer had trained under my father and later worked as his junior. In later years, he became an ardent devotee of Sri Aurobindo, and having donated all his assets to the ashram, shifted there with his family. He was a descendant of Veenai Kuppayyar, a direct disciple of Tyagaraja. A deeply religious man, he was cultured and well-versed in music. He was a major donor to the Congress and also a great support to the national poet Subramania Bharati. Sri Viswanathan[125], who had served as Governor of Kerala, was his elder son-in-law. Doraiswami Iyer was greatly devoted to my father, so he showered love and affection on my brother as he would have on his own son.

My mother was diagnosed with a stomach tumour and had to be operated upon, after which she became very weak. My responsibilities began to increase. Earlier, I was never enthusiastic about domestic chores and performed

---

[124]Sayanapuram Doraiswami Iyer (1882–1976) was Advocate General of the Madras High Court.
[125]V. Viswanathan was an ICS who, after retirement, became Governor of Kerala in the 1960s.

them only at my mother's bidding. But following my reading of Gandhiji's essays in *Young India*, I realized the virtues of physical work and service to others. I frequently began pondering over how I ought not to be a burden to others following my own life failures. I concluded that I could compensate only by performing my duties to the best extent possible and became immersed in them.

As my father was deeply involved in Congress matters, there was a great influx of guests from time to time at our house. Congress leaders from North India invariably stayed with us. Organizing everything for them, from meals onwards, was under my mother's supervision. I assisted her. As I became increasingly involved in various activities, the worries that were plaguing my heart abated, and I attained a degree of peace.

As domestic happiness was denied to me, I had to find a new direction to my life. In the olden days, women who had been denied familial happiness became renunciates, spent their life in the pursuit of spirituality, worship and going on pilgrimages. I desired to dedicate my life to the service of the nation and society. After all, is it not necessary for every human to have some goal in life?

A Pandemic

An hitherto unheard-of illness swept through the nation at the end of World War I. It was influenza[126]. The red

---

[126]Spanish influenza, which began in 1918, lasted for three years and

poppy flower from which opium is extracted began to grow profusely in Belgium, where many soldiers had been killed just a year earlier. Scientists opined that influenza originated from poppy-laden air and spread the world over[127]. Doctors initially struggled to treat the disease. Everyone in our household, except my father and I, was afflicted. My son Krishnaswami had a high fever and was treated by Dr Sitapati[128] who was considered an expert in the field. Thereafter, he became our family physician. Those were times when over-the-counter medication was not available. Doctors wrote out prescriptions, and the medication was then prepared in pharmacies.

I think it was in 1921, when Gandhiji camped at the San Thome residence of Ramji Kalyanji[129], that many women, including my aunt Janammal and me, called on him. He asked us to spin khadi, join the Congress and collect funds for the Tilak Swarajya Fund. We decided to act accordingly.

As my mother's health became a cause for some

---

infected over 500 million people worldwide.

[127]This is not correct. The poppy was the first flower to bloom in the battlefields after the war and so remains associated with it. The influenza was caused by a virus whose origin remains unknown.

[128]Rao Bahadur Dr T. Sitapati Iyer (1880–1954) was the first Indian to become Assistant Director of King Institute, and a prominent medical practitioner.

[129]As per accounts of Mahatma Gandhi's life, he stayed at the Ramji Kalyanji residence in Madurai in 1921. This was a prominent business family of that city. Gandhiji must have stayed elsewhere in Madras in 1921.

concern, we stopped our summer visits to Ootacamund or Kodaikanal and went instead to Bangalore, where my father purchased Gokulam, a house in Basavangudi. My mother's cousin Pankajam, who was Dewan Rangacharlu's daughter, lived close by. Her son Srinivasacharlu and my brother Parthasarathy became very close friends.

Women's Indian Association (WIA)

The Women's Indian Association was established in 1917 with the assistance of Annie Besant. Dr Muthulakshmi Reddy[130], Mrs Margaret Cousins[131] and Mrs Dorothy Jinarajadasa[132] founded this institution and ran it. Dr Muthulakshmi Reddy, Sister Subbalakshmi[133] and Rukmini Lakshmipathi[134] can be considered the first educated women of South India. Among them, Sister Subbalakshmi was a child widow. Her father, being a high-placed official in the education department, got her

---

[130] Dr Muthulakshmi Reddy (1886–1968) was a medical practitioner and a social reformer.

[131] Margaret Gillespie (1878–1954) married noted poet and critic James Cousins, became a Theosophist, and was later involved in the Indian freedom movement.

[132] Dorothy Graham (1882–1963) was a Scotswoman and a noted suffragette who was married to Sri Lankan Theosophist C. Jinarajadasa.

[133] R.S. Subbalakshmi (1886–1969), an educationist and a social reformer, did much to improve the condition of Brahmin widows.

[134] Rukmini Lakshmipathi (1892–1951) was a freedom fighter and the first woman member of the Madras Legislature, and later, the first woman minister of the Madras Presidency.

to qualify with a BABT degree, despite opposition from the orthodox.

On graduation, Sister Subbalakshmi did not consider her achievement noteworthy. She wanted other Brahmin girls to qualify like herself, and worked hard as an educationist. Apart from being headmistress at Lady Willingdon High School and Presidency Secondary and Teachers' Training School, she struggled to establish a widows' home. Many young widows began receiving a stipend from the government and joined the widows' home located at Ice House[135] in Thiruvallikeni, and began training as teachers. Sister Subbalakshmi's aunt, who was also a child widow, became the matron of this home.

Not content with this, Sister Subbalakshmi started the Sarada Ladies' Union in Big Street, in the Thiruvallikeni area. Under its auspices, she began a school where destitute women, those abandoned by their husbands, and child widows, could train as teachers. They qualified as higher elementary grade teachers and you can see them even now all over South India, working at various schools. As women teachers were hard to come by till then, Sister Subbalakshmi came in for praise from the government and the public.

Padma Bhushan Dr Muthulakshmi Reddy was of the same age as Sister Subbalakshmi. She was born into a

---

[135] A prominent landmark on the Marina beachfront, it gets its name from being constructed for storing ice imported from the USA in the nineteenth century. It is now a museum dedicated to Swami Vivekananda.

Brahmin family[136] of Pudukottai. Her father being highly qualified made sure his daughter became a doctor. She married Dr Sundara Reddy as per Brahmo Samaj rites.

In those days, no other Hindu woman had qualified as a doctor. Dr Muthulakshmi, therefore, became the gynaecologist for the women of well-known families in Mylapore and Thiruvallikeni. Her husband and she were greatly motivated by a desire for *seva* (selfless service) and reform, so they focused more on the upliftment of women than on their medical practice.

Rukmini was the daughter of a well-known Rao family of Thiruvallikeni. She married Ayurvedic practitioner Dr Lakshmipathi in a reformist ceremony. She was a graduate and later joined the Congress. She was minister for health in the Prakasam ministry[137].

Many women Theosophists joined the Women's Indian Association, which had women's rights as its primary goal. It worked to ensure they had access to higher education, jobs and votes. It also worked ceaselessly to champion the Sarda Bill which sought to raise the marriageable age for women, and also other proposals such as the bill against polygamy, the Anti-Nautch Bill[138] and women's divorce rights and right to property.

---

[136] Not entirely correct. Dr Reddy's father was a Brahmin while the mother was a Devadasi.

[137] This was a short-lived Congress government under the leadership of T. Prakasam. It lasted from March 1946 to March 1947.

[138] Legislation brought in by Dr Muthulakshmi Reddy to ban the dedicating girls to temples, a practice known as the Devadasi system.

The All India Women's Conference

The Madras Women's Indian Association created the All India Women's Conference. The latter, with membership across India, became an active body. It held annual conventions which were attended by members from all over the country. Resolutions were passed in support of various bills detailed earlier and sent to central and provincial governments. The members also met in person the ministers responsible. Articles on its activities appeared in the press, and soon it became a body hugely respected in official circles. In the North, members such as Rajkumari Amrit Kaur[139], Rameswari Nehru[140], Sarojini Naidu[141], Kamaladevi Chattopadhyay[142], Rani Rajwade[143], Lakshmi Menon[144], and others worked hard to convert these bills into acts of law. South Indian women supported all the proposals other than the one on divorce.

My mother and I, along with the women of other

---

[139] Rajkumari Amrit Kaur (1887–1964) was a freedom fighter and also independent India's first health minister.

[140] Rameshwari Nehru (1886–1966) was a prominent social worker.

[141] Sarojini Naidu (1879–1949), a prominent freedom fighter and poet, known as the Nightingale of India, was the first governor of Uttar Pradesh post-Independence.

[142] Kamaladevi Chattopadhyay (1903–88) was a freedom fighter, and a champion of Indian craft and theatre.

[143] Lakshmibai Rajwade (1887–1984) was a social reformer, suffragette, doctor and an advocate of family planning.

[144] Lakshmi N. Menon (1899–1994) was a freedom fighter and a union minister of state in the 1960s.

prominent Mylapore families, participated in the meetings of the All India Women's Conference and spoke in support of the resolutions. It can be said that even women from orthodox families and those who were young, though not present, extended to us their silent support.

Members of the Brahmo Samaj, established by Raja Ram Mohan Roy[145], and those of the Arya Samaj too extended their support. The former organization was responsible for the outlawing of sati—the North Indian practice of women burning themselves on the pyre of their husbands. It also championed the cause of intercommunity marriages and widow remarriage.

One of the goals of the Arya Samaj was granting women equal right to education. It sought to grant women the right to the sacred thread, thereby opening the door to the chanting of the Gayatri Mantra, and also their right to perform Vedic and religious ceremonies. Dayananda Saraswati[146], founder of the Arya Samaj, established several *gurukul*s exclusively for women all over North India, where women received both education and spiritual training.

The bill to outlaw child marriages was introduced by Har Bilas Sarda[147], so it came to be known as the Sarda

---

[145]Raja Ram Mohan Roy (1772–1833) was a social reformer.
[146]Swami Dayananda Saraswati (1824–1883), born Mool Shankar Tiwari, was a philosopher and a social reformer.
[147]Dewan Bahadur Har Bilas Sarda (1867–1955) was an academic, a judge and politician.

Bill. A group in North India known as the Sanatana Dharmishtas and orthodox Brahmins in South India bitterly opposed this. The whole country was discussing nothing else before the bill became an act, and in the year prior to its implementation, thousands of child marriages were conducted.

The next bill to become a law in favour of women was concerned with banning the degrading practice of dedicating them to temples and referring to them as Devadasis thereafter. The credit for this proposal must go to Dr Muthulakshmi Reddy. The pontiffs of various religious establishments and most men were against it, but given the support it had from women, it soon became a law.

Within a few years after these two acts, the Women's Indian Association sought legislation against polygamy. Initially, the proposal faced stiff opposition from both men and women. This was chiefly owing to divorce being a part of the bill. Even learned men such as Rajaji[148] and Satyamurti opposed it. If only the clauses concerning divorce had not been a part of it, all would have been well, but legal experts opined that the bill could not be passed without those clauses. My father looked into the matter, and based on a few amendments that he brought in, Dr Mrs Reddy with great effort introduced the bill

---

[148]Referred to variously as C. Rajagopalachari and Chakravarti Rajagopalachari/Rajagopalachariar, but most often as Rajaji, he (1878–1972) was a prominent freedom fighter who later became the last Governor-General of India.

which soon became a law. Women readily accepted this amended act.

By this time, several new members such as Radhabai Subbaroyan[149] and Ammu Swaminadhan[150] had joined the Women's Indian Association. Lady Venkatasubba Rao[151] was already a member. She began a school under the auspices of the Women's Indian Association at Royapettah, where women were educated and also given vocational training in tailoring. This now functions as the Seva Sadan[152].

Dr Reddy began many institutions for women and children's welfare under the auspices of the Women's Indian Association. Some of these include the Children's Aid Society, the Vigilance Home and the Avvai Home. Finally, she also established the Cancer Institute at Adyar. I consider the Padma Bhushan conferred on her by Government of India to be an apt honour.

---

[149]Radhabai Subbarayan (1891–1960) was the wife of Dr P. Subbarayan, sometime chief minister of Madras. She was a social reformer and a freedom fighter.

[150]Ammu Swaminadhan (1894–1978), a social reformer and a freedom fighter, was among the first women councillors of the Madras Corporation, and later Member of the Constituent Assembly.

[151]Lady Andal (1894–1969) was the wife of Sir M. Venkatasubba Rao, a judge of the Madras High Court, and later, Agent of the Nizam of Hyderabad and Berar. She was a social reformer.

[152]It presently functions from Harrington Road.

Gandhiji at My Home

Gandhiji's mission was to create a new India with a vibrant economy and a society with no divisions. In his *Young India* magazine, he had spelt out his vision—people of the country had to have an insatiable thirst for its unity and freedom. They had to work tirelessly for this with simplicity, discipline, love for service, sacrifice, patriotism, endurance, honesty and fearlessness. Gandhiji's plans for the nation, his Civil Disobedience Movement, and his public utterances enraged the British. They began to fear this would bring to an end their rule over India. As a consequence, they began to implement very repressive measures. There were *lathi* charges all over the country and prisons began to fill up. Leaders such as Tilak were exiled[153]. Gandhiji was imprisoned!

His voice, however, was heard all over the country, and his battle for Satyagraha gained momentum. This was when circumstances so arranged themselves that the Muslims too began to participate in the freedom movement. They wanted their demands concerning the Khilafat Movement[154] to be included in the Congress agenda, so they became part of the Satyagraha Movement. Muslim leaders such as Shaukat Ali, Mohammed Ali

---

[153]This is chronologically incorrect. Tilak had died by then. He had been imprisoned at Mandalay in 1908 for six years.

[154]The Khilafat Movement demanded the return of the Caliph to the throne of the Ottoman Empire after World War I. This was led by Mohammed Ali and Shaukat Ali.

and Jinnah[155] joined the Congress. Many Harijan brothers joined the movement and worked with my father. People from all backgrounds began calling at our home. Many leaders from North India came to stay. Food arrangements had to be made for everyone night and day. With that, in keeping with Congress's principles, we too dropped all religion and caste-based differentiations at home. Thereafter, all dinners at home saw people of all castes and religions sitting together at meals. Though she was of an orthodox bent of mind, my mother followed my father. Except for the puja room and the kitchen, she permitted guests to wander around at will. But women were still not permitted to mix freely with men.

For those from the North, my mother and I would prepare food such as puri, chapati and dal, and have them served by the cook. I was quite amazed at the etiquette of these visitors. When they took leave of my father, they always made it a point to call on my mother and seek her blessings. Those were days when I did not participate directly in politics. But I was a four-anna member of the Congress. I spun the charkha (spinning wheel) and learnt Hindi. My father, who thus far had always addressed the public in English, had to speak in Tamil after joining the Congress. Following his lead, I,

---

[155]Mohammed Ali Jinnah (1876–1948) was a brilliant lawyer from Bombay, who later became a member of the Congress, and still later, joined the Muslim League and engineered the creation of Pakistan, becoming its Governor-General.

who had thus far written letters to friends and relatives in English, switched over to Tamil.

Gandhiji and Kasturba came to Madras in 1925, en route to Thiruvananthapuram. This was when the Vaikom Satyagraha[156], in connection with the temple entry, was going on. They stayed at my home for three days. On their previous visit, we had held a reception for them in the garden. This time, we invited Gandhiji in, seated him on a mattress of khaddar and literally worshipped him. Why this change? Well, Gandhiji too had transformed. Then he was a civil rights activist owing to his role in the South African civil rights movement. Now he was a role model—a man who had sacrificed his life for the sake of the country!

All through the day, people came to see him. One devotee came with his six-year-old daughter. Gandhiji placed her on his lap and began conversing with her. He saw her gold bangles and asked, 'Child, will you give them to me?' She immediately said yes and then looked at her father. Everyone was watching in stunned silence. 'Please give Gandhi Thaatha your bangles,' said the father. Gandhiji was a master at begging for what he wanted. He immediately began to slip the bangles off the girl's hands. But it was not so easy. 'Get a pair

---

[156]The Vaikom Satyagraha centred on the demand for free access of all people irrespective of caste to the four streets surrounding the Mahadeva Temple in Vaikom. The agitation took place in 1924/1925 and saw the involvement of several social reformers including Sree Narayana Guru, Periyar E.V. Ramaswami and Mahatma Gandhi.

of pliers,' he declared! I, who was watching this with other women, was somewhat annoyed with the Mahatma. I quickly went indoors and placed the pearl necklace I was wearing in the safe.

On one of the three days of their stay, we organized a special meeting for women, to be presided over by Kasturba at Vasantha Bungalow[157] in Thiruvallikeni. She gave a brief speech in Hindi. At her request, all the women led by Kothainayaki Ammal[158] donated their jewellery to fund the cause. This was the first time the women of Madras donated their jewellery for a noble cause. From then onwards, Gandhiji spoke highly of South Indian women and commended their willingness to sacrifice. I must add here that it was Gandhiji who reduced to a great extent the craze Indian women had for jewellery.

During his stay with us, Gandhiji was reading Katherine Mayo's book *Mother India*. The author, an American, had written very derogatively and in a biased manner about Indian women. She had described them as brainless, uneducated, bound to the kitchen, and unaware of the outside world. She had also written that Indians were not qualified to become independent. The Mahatma described the book as a sanitary inspector's report in an article in *Young India*. He asked me if I had

---

[157] The Spring Pavilion around the temple tank, where the deity is brought on ceremonial occasions.
[158] Vai Mu Kothainayaki Ammal (1901–60) was a pioneering Tamil woman novelist, publisher, freedom fighter, singer and an orator.

read it. When I said no, he gave it to me and asked me to read it and give my opinion on it by nightfall. When he asked me my views the next day, I said that though it was largely nonsense, there were some home truths in it. He said it was his view that educated women like me ought to work to eradicate the faults highlighted in the work. Mayo's book and the Mahatma's opinion of it gave me a new goal in life—that of social service.

Gandhiji observed silence on Mondays, and on one of those evenings, he was seated on the first floor, engaged in writing articles for *Young India*. Some of those present asked me to play the *veena*. While I was doing so, a note came from the Mahatma. I was stunned to read what he had written: 'You may think being immersed in work, I am not paying attention to your performance. But I am listening to it even as I write.' I was overcome by embarrassment.

Mahadev Desai[159], who was nearby, asked me if I understood the lyrics and import of the songs I played. How was I to tell him that I did not know anything of the Tyagaraja[160] and Dikshitar[161] compositions I performed!

The three days the Mahatma stayed with us went by in a flash. All my time was spent observing Gandhiji:

---

[159]Mahadev Haribhai Desai (1892–1942) was a freedom fighter best remembered for being Mahatma Gandhi's secretary.
[160]Tyagaraja (1767–1847) was a composer of Carnatic music, largely in the Telugu language.
[161]Muthuswami Dikshitar (1775–1835) was a composer of Carnatic music, largely in Sanskrit.

what he did, noting where he was going, attending to his wants, and watching how he spoke and laughed. When he left, I was completely rudderless. It appeared as though life had come to a halt. I wandered around the house. I treasured every object he had used and considered them articles of worship. A great joy permeated by sorrow filled my being.

That year, in the month of April, my brother's wife gave birth to a daughter. According to my father's wishes, she was named Vasanthi, after C.R. Das's wife. My son continued to be plagued by illnesses. Western medical practice recommended feeding the child every three hours but Indian nurses fed him whenever he cried. Child rearing is a difficult art that every woman ought to be trained in.

First Struggle Ends in Failure

Despite joining the Congress, differences of opinion over various matters persisted between my father and Gandhiji. But he greatly venerated the latter and always spoke admiringly of him. He accompanied him to Vaikom as well. But he did not believe in courting imprisonment. 'I will continue my fight for independence without going to jail as far as possible,' he declared often. 'But I will remain unshaken if the government decides to arrest me.'

That year, there was a split in the Congress. The Swarajya Party, a faction within the Congress, came into existence under the leadership of Motilal Nehru and C.R. Das in the North, and under S. Srinivasa Iyengar (my father), A. Rangaswami Iyengar[162] and Satyamurti in the South. They were of the view that the Civil Disobedience Movement alone could not vouchsafe independence, and that it was necessary for the Congress to participate in the Provincial and Central Legislatures, and thereby fight the British government from within. Others such as Rajaji opposed the entry of the Congress into the legislatures and were branded as no-changers. This included Gandhiji as well. They worked on several projects aimed at strengthening the Party.

In 1920, while the Mahatma's Civil Disobedience Movement was at its peak, a few Congress workers attacked a police station at Chauri Chaura, and set it on fire. Four policemen were killed in the conflagration. On learning of this horrific incident, Mahatma Gandhi said that he realized that the Congress had not yet attained maturity in non-violence as a creed. He said he had committed a Himalayan blunder by starting the Civil Disobedience Movement and immediately called it off. He, however, asked the party to continue with its constructive activities and its service to Harijans. People like Rajaji began to focus on these.

Similarly, a short while after Annie Besant began the Home Rule Movement, there was a split within the

---

[162]A. Rangaswami Iyengar (1877–1934) was a freedom fighter, Member of the Central Legislature, and Chief Editor of *The Hindu.*

Congress. The moderates included the likes of Annie Besant, Gokhale, Jayakar, Dr S. Subramania Iyer and the Right Honourable V.S. Srinivasa Sastri[163]. Motilal Nehru, Gandhiji, Lajpat Rai, Tilak and C.R. Das were the extremists.

Rise of the Justice Party

Based on the divide between Brahmins and non-Brahmins, the Justice Party[164], a new entity, came into existence in South India. At the forefront were leaders such as Patro[165], Panneerselvam[166], Theyagaroya Chettiyar[167],

---

[163] The Right Honourable V.S. Srinivasa Sastri (1869–1946) was an educationist, a silver-tongued orator, Member of the Servants of India Society, a moderate, and Member of the Imperial Legislative Council.
[164] Officially, the South Indian Liberation Front and founded in 1917, it was better known as the Justice Party after the eponymous newspaper it promoted.
[165] Sir Aneppu Parasuramdas Patro (1875–1946) was an Odisha-based aristocrat who also spearheaded the movement to declare that area as a separate province from the Madras Presidency. He was a minister in the Justice Cabinet from 1921 to 1926 and later speaker of the Odisha Legislative Assembly.
[166] Sir A.T. Panneerselvam (1888–1940) was the leader of the Justice Party and later a minister in its various cabinets.
[167] Sir Pitty Theyagaroya Chetty (1852–1925) was one of the founders of the Justice Party and later the first Indian to become president of the Madras Corporation. T. Nagar commemorates him.

Vande Mataram

Dr Subbaroyan[168], Sankaran Nair, the Panagal Raja[169] and Sir P.T. Rajan[170]. The party opined that under the British, the Brahmins had cleverly managed to rise. Since the community had a number of qualified vakils, senior positions in the government had all been filled by its members. This is why, the Justice Party felt, the non-Brahmins had remained backward. It sought reservation on the basis of caste and religion and on that basis, fought and won elections to the Corporation Council and the Madras Legislative Council. Having filled these positions, the Justice Party worked hard towards ensuring that non-Brahmins obtained several concessions.

After World War I, the Central and Provincial Legislatures came into existence. The Swarajists brought a proposal to the Congress Session that candidates from the party would be fielded henceforth in the City, Provincial and Central Legislatures. This was duly passed. At that time, my father headed the Madras Provincial Congress,

---

[168]Dr P. Subbaroyan (1889–1962) was the hereditary zamindar of Kumaramangalam, and not a member of the Justice Party. Being independent, he was selected as a compromise chief minister of Madras from 1926 to 1930 when no party had a majority. Later, he joined the Congress and was union minister post-Independence and also Ambassador of India to Indonesia. He was the husband of Radhabai.

[169]Sir Panaganti Ramarayaningar (1866–1928), Rajah of Panagal, was zamindar of Kalahasti and later prime minister of Madras between 1921 and 1928. Panagal Park commemorates him.

[170]Sir Ponnambalam Thiagarajan (1892–1974) was minister and later prime minister of Madras in the 1930s. He was the last president of the Justice Party.

and he began selecting candidates for the elections to the Provincial Legislature.

During the elections, the atmosphere at our house cannot be described. My father was out the whole day, addressing meetings where he held forth on the Congress and its principles. I, too, went and solicited the women's votes. There were meetings where clashes between the Congress and Justice Party supporters took place, with instances of stone throwing. But, by and large, the welcome the Congress received wherever we went was overwhelming. My brother, his friends V.K. Thiruvenkatachari[171], Salem Vijayaraghavachari[172], Varadachari, who was called Kasi[173], R. Varadachari, and T.T. Krishnamachari[174] helped out with the campaigning. Throughout this time, there was not a single stay-at-home male. The phone kept ringing all day. If we answered, we received a barrage of abuse from those in the opposition party. Threatening anonymous letters flowed to our address. My father was unfazed but my mother and I

---

[171] V.K. Thiruvenkatachari (1904–84) was a junior in law to S. Srinivasa Iyengar, and later, a leading lawyer of Madras and Advocate General, Government of Madras.

[172] Salem C. Vijayaraghavachariar (1852–1944), a leading lawyer of the Salem Bar, framed the Swaraj Constitution of India, and was president of the Congress in 1920.

[173] N.D. Varadachariar, aka Kasi (1903–45), was a short-lived but brilliant lawyer remembered today for his detailed diary entries.

[174] T.T. Krishnamachari (1899–1974) was a leading businessman, and later, member of the Constituent Assembly and union minister, Government of India.

were quite worried. He would return home late every night, and we would remain awake till he came back.

Taking care of coffee and tiffin supplies to those involved in campaigning was our responsibility. On election day, over a hundred cars were parked in our compound. Around 200 people ate at our place. Cars were sent to ferry voters to booths. The house was empty from 8.00 a.m. to 6.00 p.m. All the Congress candidates placed by my father won. The Justice Party was defeated.

My grandmother, Lady Bhashyam Iyengar, passed away in 1926 after an illness lasting two months. She was 81. Lakshmi Vilas was rented out as my uncle Venuswami had shifted with his family to Madurai. My aunt Janammal, having stayed with her elder brother for a few days, built a house on Moubray's Road and shifted there.

My Father at the Central Legislature, Delhi

Shafi Mohammed, Ameed Khan[175], Chakkarai Chetty[176] and Muthuranga Mudaliar[177] had been elected to the Corporation Council. Elections had also been held to the Provincial and Central Legislatures simultaneously. Satyamurti was elected to the former and my father to the latter. With this victory for the Congress in the Madras

---

[175] Abdul Hameed Khan (1892–1965) was later Mayor of Madras.

[176] V. Chakkarai Chetty (1880–1958), Labour leader who was also a member of the Congress, was later Mayor of Madras.

[177] C.N. Muthuranga Mudaliar (1888–1949) was a Chengalpattu-based aristocrat, an active Congressman and a freedom fighter.

Presidency, my father's fame spread everywhere. He was elected President of the Congress session at Gauhati which took place in 1926.

Gandhiji and Ba stayed at our house once again, en route to Ceylon. I saw the women volunteers and leaders who came with him and had a great desire to go along with them to Ceylon. I pleaded with my father for permission but he remained unmoved. My request to go with him to Gauhati was met with the same response.

My father and Motilal Nehru having been elected to the Central Legislature in Delhi, our family shifted there for three months each year, when it was in session. It was only then that I could comprehend the deep divide between Hindus and Muslims. In my early days there, I struggled to identify who was Hindu and who Muslim. Everyone seemed to dress, walk, and talk the same way. I assumed that all veiled women were Muslims and asked one lady who was dressed that way if she was one. The response was a vehement and angry denial and a firm declaration that she was a Hindu. I was stunned at the hatred in her reply.

During the Civil Disobedience Movement, Muslim leaders such as Shaukat Ali, Mohammed Ali and Jinnah joined the Congress to press for the Khilafat demand. They began leaving the party in later years, owing to differences of opinion, and thus was born the Muslim League. My father tried his best to resolve the differences but it was all to no avail. The main reason for this divide was the Hindu Mahasabha managing to

A rare photograph of a smiling Ambujammal, circa 1940s
(*Courtesy Srinivasa Gandhi Nilayam*)

Sir V. Bhashyam Iyengar, Ambujammal's maternal grandfather
(*translator's personal collection*)

Sriman Srinivasa Iyengar, Ambujammal's father
(*translator's personal collection*)

Ranganayaki Ammal, Ambujammal's mother
(*Courtesy Srinivasa Gandhi Nilayam*)

Lakshmi Vilas, where Ambujammal's maternal grandparents lived
(*Courtesy The Buchi Babu family*)

Amjad Bagh, the house that Sriman Srinivasa Iyengar acquired
(*translator's personal collection*)

सेवाग्राम SEVAGRAM, سیواگرام
वर्धा सी.पी. WARDHA, C.P. وردہا سی۔ پی

14-6-41

Chi. Ambujam,

I have your
descriptive letter.
I can well under-
stand your &
mother's grief.
Have I not personally
known what a
domestic man
father was. His
love for you all
was boundless
His love of the

A letter from Mahatma Gandhi to Ambujammal
(*Courtesy Srinivasa Gandhi Nilayam*)

Ambujammal (standing in the middle and holding a flag) with other picketers of shops selling foreign goods
(*translator's personal collection*)

Ambujammal (seated second from left and wearing glasses), along with Dr Muthulakshmi Reddy (seated centre), at a prayer meet
(*translator's personal collection*)

Ambujammal welcomes P.S. Kumarasamy Raja, chief minister of Madras State, at an event circa early 1950s
(*Courtesy Srinivasa Gandhi Nilayam*)

Ambujammal at the forefront of a pandal welcomes delegates to the Avadi Congress session, 1955
(*Courtesy Srinivasa Gandhi Nilayam*)

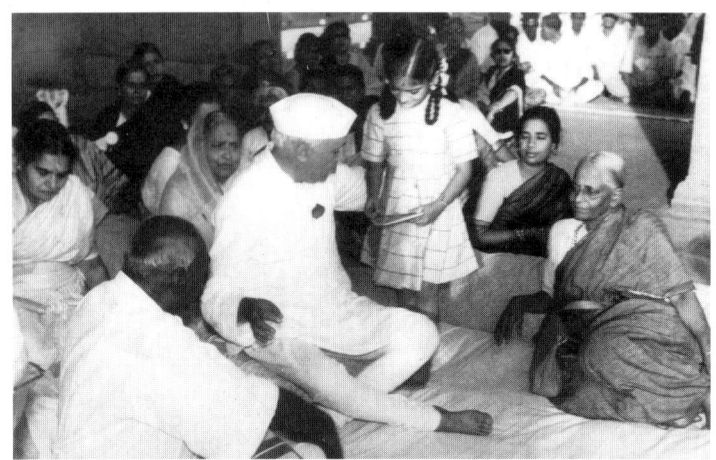

K. Kamaraj (back to camera), Pt Jawaharlal Nehru and Ambujammal at the Avadi Congress
(*Courtesy Srinivasa Gandhi Nilayam*)

Ambujammal receives the Padma Shri from the then President of India Sarvepalli Radhakrishnan
(*Courtesy Srinivasa Gandhi Nilayam*)

At the condolence meet on the passing of Ambujammal
(*Courtesy Srinivasa Gandhi Nilayam*)

Srinivasa Gandhi Nilayam today
(*Photo by William Satish*)

Ambujammal's brother Parthasarathy (left) with the Vaishnavi idol he worshipped
(*Courtesy Srinivasa Gandhi Nilayam*)

The tulsi planter at Srinivasa Gandhi Nilayam that contains some of Mahatma Gandhi's ashes
(*Photo by William Satish*)

Ambujammal's photo that welcomes visitors to Srinivasa Gandhi Nilayam today
(*Courtesy Srinivasa Gandhi Nilayam*)

Vande Mataram

get Motilal Nehru to include some of their demands in the Congress resolutions. Hindu-Muslim riots erupted all over the country.

Even before the time of Chhatrapati Shivaji, the Sikhs, and later the Arya Samajis were stern opponents of the Muslims. Disturbances of a communal nature were common in the frontier areas, especially in the Punjab province. Rumours were rife that Hindu women were being abducted by Muslims.

Swami Shraddhanand[178], who was a well-known Arya Samaj sannyasi[179], was universally respected. He and Swami Dayananda Saraswati propounded several measures for the uplift of women. Many institutions were established for imparting higher education to women, and for the abolition of the *purdah*. Apart from academics, students here were trained in self-defence, firearms, and exercise using clubs, dumb bells and staffs.

Swami Shraddhanand once visited Madras and my father invited him home. He looked like a sage. We prostrated before him, offered fruits and milk, and received his blessings. Two months before the Gauhati Congress, when the Swami was in a library in Delhi, a young Muslim entered pretending to want to meet him, and shouting that the Swami was against all Muslims, shot him dead. A grand procession of elephants had been planned for the Gauhati Congress that my father was

---

[178] Swami Shraddhanand (Mahatma Munshi Ram Vij, 1856–1926) was a freedom fighter and a social reformer.

[179] He was not a founder of the Arya Samaj but a prominent member.

to preside over. But in view of the sad killing of Swami Shraddhanand, my father asked for it to be cancelled.

My father wanted the subsequent Congress session to be held in Madras, and he travelled from town to town raising funds for the party to make the event possible. The session, held at Spur Tank[180] in Egmore in December 1927, was under the presidentship of Hakim Ajmal Khan[181]. Muthuranga Mudaliar was the chairman of the welcoming committee. It was in this session that the demand for *Purna Swaraj* or total independence was passed. Till then, Gandhiji, Motilal Nehru and a few others had felt that dominion status was enough for us. But Jawahar[182], Subhash[183], my father and other young people felt that only total independence would do. The resolution was passed with overwhelming support, leading to several divisions within the Congress.

I did not participate in the Congress session held in Madras as I was in a state of depression, weeping and laughing to myself. The doctors diagnosed this as hysteria, and to affect a cure, I went with my mother to

---

[180] A water body that existed in Egmore and is commemorated by the name of a road. Today, the TB Institute stands in its place.
[181] Hakim Ajmal Khan (1868–1927) was a physician and an educationist.
[182] Pandit Jawaharlal Nehru (1889–1964) was a freedom fighter and independent India's first prime minister.
[183] Netaji Subhas Chandra Bose (1899–1945) was a freedom fighter and Founder of the Indian National Army, which led the Azad Hind movement to free India with German and Japanese help during World War II.

Tirukutralam[184] for two months. The change of place and the daily baths in the waterfall restored me to normalcy. I was at peace with myself. Returning home, I was raring to do something, but having no education or experience, I did not know what to do. I joined the Sarada Vidyalaya run by Sister Subbalakshmi in Thiruvallikeni and trained as a higher-grade teacher. When the school shifted to Padma Vilas in Luz, I worked as a teacher for six months.

In 1928, the Simon Commission[185] came to India, ostensibly to study Indian views on independence. It was slated to travel all over the country, and the Congress decided to boycott it. As soon as the members of the Commission arrived, they were met with protests. In Punjab, a massive gathering was organized under the leadership of Lala Lajpat Rai. The police, in order to break this up, conducted a lathi charge in which Lalaji was grievously injured in the chest. He was bedridden for a few days and then died.

When the Commission came to Madras, a massive protest march was organized under the leadership of my father. Bulusu Sambamurthy[186], leader of the Andhra Congress Committee, and Muthuranga Mudaliar, head

---

[184] A village in Tirunelveli District, known as Courtallam, famed for its waterfalls and salubrious climate.

[185] Headed by Sir John Simon, with seven Members of Parliament, it was officially known as the Indian Statutory Commission. Set up to study constitutional reform in India, it was opposed as there was not one Indian in it.

[186] Bulusu Sambamurthy (1886–1958) was a lawyer and a freedom fighter.

of the Madras Presidency Congress Committee, also participated. While it was passing through Rattan Bazaar[187], the police commissioner came and said he wished to speak to my father. The procession was halted while the two conversed. The police commissioner said that if the procession proceeded any further, the police would have no option but to resort to lathi charge. 'For the sake of public peace, we appeal to you not to go any further,' he said. 'Don't unnecessarily cause bloodshed. By conducting the procession thus far, you have already brought to the notice of the authorities your opposition to the Simon Commission. It is of no purpose to take this any further.'

My father felt the police commissioner was speaking sense. He ordered the crowds to disperse. However, this was not to the liking of people such as Bulusu Sambamurthy. They branded my father as someone who was afraid of lathi charges, and of antagonizing the British. But my father could not care less. He was not swayed by the views of others and did only what he felt was correct. 'Courage is one thing; foolhardiness is entirely another,' he would often say. He never wavered from the principle that it was futile to court fame and popularity by subjecting oneself and others to difficulties.

At the Lahore Congress, the youth wing once again brought forth the Purna Swaraj resolution, and there was

---

[187] A commercial district of North Madras.

considerable difference of opinion leading to Jawahar, Subhash and my father staging a walkout. They formed themselves into the Forward Bloc, an entity within the Congress. This was not to the liking of Motilal Nehru. He convinced his son Jawahar to dissolve the Forward Bloc. Once this was done, it was decided that an all-party meet would be called and the views of everyone taken. The Purna Swaraj resolution was reaffirmed at this meet, and it was also recommended that a report on this may be released. A committee headed by Motilal Nehru was formed. My father was selected as a member. He spelt out his views on the need for Hindu-Muslim unity, and his suggestions for this as well as those for the country's welfare were adopted.

Father's Foreign Trip

My father embarked on his first tour of the Western nations in 1928. Despite our entreaties to take a cook or a secretary with him, he refused and went alone. He travelled to England, Italy, France and Germany. In Ireland, he met with the freedom fighter de Valera[188] and formed a friendship. Then, at the invitation of Russian leaders, he went to that country as well. When he returned after three months, there was a great shock awaiting him.

---

[188]Eamon de Valera (1882–1975) was an Irish Republican leader.

The Nehru Report and Father's Resignation

My father discovered to his extreme disappointment that in the final version of the Nehru Report, not one of his suggestions had been incorporated. He felt that there was no benefit to the country because of the Nehru Report and that, on the contrary, there could be severe complications because of it in future. He already knew there were some Congress leaders who were staunchly opposed to his views. He also felt Mahatma Gandhi favoured only the opinions of those leaders over his. He, therefore, came to the conclusion that there was no point in remaining in an organization that did not accord his views any respect. Ignoring everyone's entreaties, he resigned from the Congress.

There were other reasons also for his resignation. One was his feeling that Gandhiji was bringing in religion-related clauses into Congress resolutions, thereby causing an increase in the friction between Hindus and Muslims. The other was an angry letter he had received from Gandhiji, accusing him of misleading the youth.

Many Congress leaders felt that Father's exit was a grievous blow to the country's freedom struggle. Several attempts were made to get him back, but all in vain. Later, Gandhiji himself sent Nehru and afterwards Mirabehn[189] to resolve the differences with Father, but the discussions were fruitless.

---

[189] Mirabehn aka Madeleine Slade (1892–1982) was an ardent follower of Mahatma Gandhi.

Dandi March

The freedom struggle once again intensified in 1929–30. Gandhiji launched the Salt Satyagraha and his famed Dandi March began in North India. Thousands followed him. Sarojini Naidu and he were sent to prison for breaking the salt laws.

In the South, a group marched to Vedaranyam (Kodikkarai) under the leadership of Chakravarti Rajagopalachari. He and Rukmini Lakshmipathi were imprisoned for this. In Madras, a volunteer camp was begun under the name of Udayavanam by E. Krishna Iyer[190]. A 16-year-old girl from Andhra and her mother had joined it. That brave girl was Durgabai[191]. Under her leadership, a band of volunteers went to the beach in Madras and made salt. Due to this, Bulusu Sambamurthy, Tenetti Viswanadham[192], T. Prakasam[193] and several other Andhra leaders went to prison along with her.

The boycott of foreign goods continued in North India under the guidance of Kasturba. In the South as

---

[190]E. Krishna Iyer (1897–1968) was a lawyer, freedom fighter, Founding Secretary of the Music Academy, and the man who took the first steps for the adoption of classical South Indian dance by all communities.
[191]Durgabai Deshmukh (1909–81) was a lawyer, freedom fighter, Member of the Constituent Assembly, and social worker.
[192]Tenetti Viswanadham (1896–1979) was a freedom fighter and later, Member of the Madras and Andhra Legislative Assemblies.
[193]Tanguturi Prakasam (1872–1957), a lawyer and freedom fighter, referred to as Andhra Kesari, was chief minister of Madras Province in 1946, and then the first chief minister of Andhra Pradesh.

well, women picketed shops selling foreign goods and also stood in silent protest outside liquor-vending outlets.

When they got to know that Kasturba had been arrested, the women of India were by and large enraged. They began participating in protests with renewed energy. One by one, the women leaders in North India were all arrested. This included Kamala Nehru[194], Kamaladevi Chattopadhyay and Swarup Rani Nehru[195].

Youth League and Women's Swadeshi League

At that time, the Youth League came up as an organization in Tamil Nadu to assist the Congress in its propaganda activities. This was headed by Rukmini Lakshmipathi. Some of the members included R. Parthasarathy, K. Venkataraman, O.P. Ramaswami[196], T.T. Krishnamachari, N.D. Varadachari (Kasi), 'Chitra' Narayanaswami[197], my brother Parthasarathy, Acharya[198], Krishnabai[199],

---

[194]Kamala Nehru (1899–1936) was the wife of Pandit Jawaharlal Nehru, and a freedom fighter.

[195]Swarup Rani Nehru (1868–1938) was the wife of Motilal Nehru, and a freedom fighter.

[196]O.P. Ramaswami Reddy (1895–1970) was a freedom fighter and later prime minister of Madras from 1947 to 1949.

[197]S. Narayanaswamy founded a leading stockbrokering firm, Chitra & Co., in 1946.

[198]P. Sri Acharya (1886–1981) was a writer and a freedom fighter.

[199]Krishnabai Nimbkar ((1906–97) was a freedom fighter, a doctor and a women's rights activist.

Kameswari, Sakuntala, Sarojini, and Sivabhogam[200].

Krishnabai and Kameswari wished to begin a separate nationalist organization for women. They invited me and my aunt Janammal. We, along with Manjubhashini[201], joined in. This entity was to be run on Gandhiji's principles—we began publicizing the virtues of khadi, training people on spinning yarn, and also learning Hindi. P. Jagannatha Das, a person from Andhra, agreed to not only lead the group but also fund it. He was a lawyer in Madras and an ardent nationalist who helped freedom fighters in various ways. He lived in a large two-storeyed house in Singarachari Street in Thiruvallikeni. We named our outfit Women's Swadeshi League. Krishnabai and Janammal were secretaries, and I was the treasurer. Kameswari, Kamalabai, Ramabai, Smt. Indirabai, R. Krishnabai, Mrs Vasudeva Rao, Kothainayaki Ammal, Pattammal, Rukmini Ammal, Ranganayaki Ammal, and Sakkubai were members. There was a key group of members that included Manjubhashini, Radhabai Subbarayan, Ammu Swaminadhan, Mrs Margaret Cousins, Sakuntala, Sivabhogam, and Dr Shakuntala. C.N. Muthuranga Mudaliar, K. Bhashyam and M. Bhaktavatsalam[202] were our advisors and helped us out when needed.

---

[200] R. Sivabhogam Ammal (1907–66) was a freedom fighter and India's first woman auditor.
[201] S. Manjubhashini (1906–96) was a freedom fighter, a social worker and founder of the Bala Mandir.
[202] M. Bhaktavatsalam (1897–1987) was a freedom fighter and later, chief minister of Madras State.

The league operated from a space in the inner courtyard of Jagannatha Das's residence. We met at 3.00 p.m. every day and conducted classes on Hindi, spinning, block printing on khadi, and singing nationalistic songs. My father did not object to my participation in these Gandhian activities. I, therefore, participated enthusiastically. In order to give this my wholehearted attention, I quit the post of honorary teacher at Sarada Vidyalaya.

As the scope of our activities expanded alongside our membership, we shifted to a hall in a house on Big Street at a monthly rent of Rs 20. We formed a band of volunteers, named ourselves *Swayamsevikas* (volunteers), and trained in providing public service. We were present at all Congress gatherings and events, and helped maintain orderly conduct among the crowds. We also went about popularizing khaddar and selling indigenously made items. We participated in prayer meetings, women's gatherings and processions. When national leaders visited, we went to the station to welcome them and created enthusiasm among the people. During the day, we went from house to house and got people to take the oath that they would use only indigenously made items. We got their signature on a declaration to this effect. We also publicized *swadeshi* (India-made) goods in villages around the city. We placed swadeshi goods such as soaps, combs and hand mirrors in push carts and went around the streets selling these. In the evenings, we went to the beach carrying swadeshi goods displayed in trays slung from our neck and also khadi in shoulder bags.

We encouraged society ladies who came to take the air in the beach to buy our goods. If they refused, in keeping with our principles, we gave them a lecture on Gandhian thought. We had the figures of how much was being spent annually by India to purchase cloth from mills in Lancashire, Manchester and Glasgow. We shared these figures to enlighten people as to how much foreign firms were benefitting at our expense. We also served with enthusiasm at the Mahamakham Festival[203] and at exhibitions held in the city.

We had several interesting experiences as we went from street to street, propagating the boycott of foreign goods. We never reacted to all the abuse we received, and having suppressed our egos, went about our task. Gandhiji's golden words were the sole reason for our equanimity.

Wherever we went, whether within the city or outside, we did so in groups of 10. Now and then, we began getting news of women in North India being arrested for their boycott of foreign goods. When we heard of this, we too were eager to go to prison for the cause of khadi. We decided that if the need arose, we would not hesitate being jailed, and prepared ourselves for such an eventuality. We continued with our activities despite the heightened vigil of the police.

---

[203] Held once in 12 years at Kumbakonam.

Swadeshi Bhajans

Once, in the month of Margazhi (December/January), we conducted *prabhat pheri*—the singing of nationalistic songs in a chorus—early in the morning around the Thiruvallikeni Parthasarathi Temple. As this was the time when the Thiruppavai songs were sung in chorus as devotees went around the temple, our performance too received very good support. Hearing the singing of Kothainayaki Ammal's nationalistic bhajans and songs, crowds followed us. We also conducted the prabhat pheri around Kapaliswarar Temple in Mylapore for a month. The police then imposed Section 144, according to which it was forbidden for people to gather in numbers greater than four in any public space. But because we claimed to be singing the name of the Lord, nobody stopped us. At that time, Bhaktavatsalam was residing on West Mada Street. His wife Gnanasundaram Bhaktavatsalam and daughter Sarojini joined us. It was the practice of Muthuranga Mudaliar and Bhaktavatsalam to follow our bhajans. In the afternoons, we would go to Royapettah to participate in the Khadi Exhibition[204]. It was there that we got to know that both Muthuranga Mudaliar and Bhaktavatsalam would soon be arrested.

On the last day of the bhajans, at the pavilion in

---

[204]The Khadi and Swadeshi Exhibition was a regular event through the 1930s in December in Madras, at General Patters Road, on the site where the Satyamurti Bhavan, aka the Congress headquarters, stands today.

front of Kapaliswarar Temple, a public meeting was held at 9.00 a.m. under the leadership of both these men. We marked their foreheads with vermilion and wished them all success in the nationalist cause. That evening brought news of their arrest.

I Become the Third Dictator[205]

The Congress Working Committee met the next day. Following the arrests, it was resolved that I be made the third dictator of the independence movement. That evening, while I was with Janammal and others at the Congress exhibition pavilion, a senior police official took me aside and warned me that he had in his possession a warrant for my arrest. I brushed him aside and did not even consider it important to inform my parents about what had transpired. But I knew that the officer was a close acquaintance of my father's.

Some days later, a Congress leader met me and said that I was not doing enough. He wanted me to organize picketing outside shops selling foreign cloth. I replied that I needed at least a hundred women volunteers for this. He promised to organize the same and asked me to begin preparations for the picketing. True to his word,

---

[205]Though the term is offensive now, it appears that the Congress Party entrusted the administration of its regional chapters to leaders who were designated as 'Dictators'. After Muthuranga Mudaliar and Bhaktavatsalam, it would seem that Ambujammal became the third 'Dictator'.

he put together a hundred women from Gujarat, Andhra, Kerala, Tamil Nadu and other places. Srinivasan[206] of *The Hindu* gave us an old van and another donor gifted us a car to transport the volunteers.

We began picketing at places such as China Bazaar[207], Rattan Bazaar and Esplanade[208], carrying the tricolour and shouting nationalistic slogans. Young children would lead us, carrying the tricolour and chanting slogans. They were referred to as the *Vanara Sena*[209]. Male volunteers marched on either side while women, many carrying children, walked in the centre. As we marched on, singing the poems of Mahakavi Bharati with nationalistic verve, the mounted police followed us closely. Madras had never seen such processions, and crowds came to watch; the police kept driving them away. At shop entrances, owners and employees would crowd the steps to watch. When the procession ended, we branched off in pairs to picket the outlets.

We were sometimes sprayed with water or tear-gassed. But there was no violence attempted on us. The British government had clearly instructed the police to treat the

---

[206]Kasturi Srinivasan (1887–1959) was Director and Chief Editor of *The Hindu*.
[207]A commercial district of North Madras.
[208]Once a vast clearing by the sea in North Madras, it later came to house many commercial establishments.
[209]Vanara Sena—literally, army of monkeys—was inspired by the Ramayana. The Congress had child volunteers in this brigade who would participate in the freedom struggle. Indira Gandhi was among the earliest leaders of the Vanara Sena.

Indian women with due respect.

On such days, Aunt Janammal and I would leave home at 9.00 a.m. after breakfast and return only at 9.00 p.m. My mother waited anxiously for my return, and my father frequently asked if I had come home. My brother was worried as well. He too had quit the Congress, following my father's lead, but understood my feelings. Even to such an understanding brother, I did not disclose that there was a warrant for my arrest.

I Refuse to Return Home

One morning in January 1930, we were on our way to picket at Rattan Bazaar when the police officer who had warned me appeared and having arrested us, packed all of us into a lorry and took us to the Commissioner's Office. We were made to sit on wooden benches and (at government expense) were given tiffin and coffee. Krishnabai Nimbkar, her mother Kamalabai, Kameswari Ammal, Indirabai Madhav Rao, Kamalabai, R. Krishna Bai, Janammal, and Gomathi Ammal were with me. On hearing the news of their arrest, relatives of some of these women came to see them. However, nobody came from my house. The police van came at around 5.00 p.m. The names of all the women were called in turn and they boarded the vehicle. My name was omitted. Nonetheless, I went and stood by the van. Even Janammal had got into the vehicle. The van doors were shut, leaving me standing outside. 'Why have you left me out?' I shouted.

'I too participated in the picketing! I was the organizer of the protest, so I need to be arrested!' Nobody heeded me and the van left.

The police commissioner told me I could go home and he too prepared to leave office for the day. I appealed to him: 'You sent all the women who picketed along with me to prison! Why was I left out? Is this correct? I cannot remain free when they are in jail. I too need to be arrested.' He paid no attention and I was overcome with grief. I refused to leave and remained where I was.

At this time, two *satyagrahi*s (freedom fighters), Angachi Ammal and her husband, were busy preparing salt inside the Commissioner's Office campus! She assumed I was still standing there because I was afraid of going home by myself, and offered to escort me. But I refused, saying all I wanted was to be sent to prison.

Within a short while, Bhaktavatsalam and K. Bhashyam drove in and offered to take me to my home. I refused. They then invited me to stay at one of their houses instead. To this, I asked them to drop me off at Aunt Janammal's house. I declared that I resolved to continue picketing till I was arrested. Finally, I was taken to my uncle Venuswami Iyengar's house in Kilpauk, and I stayed in the first-floor room that Janammal usually occupied.

I got to know that my father had called the police commissioner over the phone and said that I was mentally ill, and so could not be sent to prison. His love for his daughter had triumphed over his love for the nation! I was very upset with him. The police commissioner had great respect for my father and obeyed him. In those days, Sriman Srinivasa Iyengar commanded great respect in government circles. Everyone heeded his words and acted accordingly.

The next morning, my parents, through the good offices of my uncle, requested me to come home, but I refused. I went to K. Bhashyam's house and requested his help in resuming my picketing activities. I also requested him to make arrangements for me to see my friends who were lodged in Central Jail[210]. He took the necessary steps and then sent me there in a car with two male volunteers and Angachi Ammal.

On reaching the prison premises, I found several relatives and friends of my jailed companions already assembled there. But nobody was permitted to meet those arrested. We got to know that owing to lack of proper food and coffee, our friends were suffering from headaches in the prison. On coming to know of this, Bhaktavatsalam and Bhashyam arranged to meet with senior prison officials and informed them that those arrested belonged to the higher strata of society, so they could not be starved in this manner. Within a couple of days, the prison authorities brought the matter before the Third Magistrate's Court, and all the women were ordered to be taken under armed escort to Vellore prison.

---

[210]Established in the 1850s and located opposite the Central Station, it was demolished in the early twenty-first century. The Madras Medical College expanded to occupy the space.

Picketing Continues

I resumed picketing from the next day at Rattan Bazaar in the company of Angachi Ammal. We sat in front of the shops selling foreign cloth, and spun the charkha. This went on from morning to evening, and a couple of male volunteers also joined us. Angachi Ammal and I would stop people from entering the shops by standing in their way with our palms pressed together. If they still attempted to go in, we gave a small but emotional speech on the condition of the Indian economy. On listening to us, the men invariably left without entering the shops. But the women! They simply pushed us aside and went ahead with their purchases, emerging later with triumphant smiles.

The shopkeepers, however, were terrified of us, and would obsequiously offer us a seat and enquire if we needed coffee or soda. Even as they were making these polite enquiries, someone inside would be telephoning the police. They would arrive in force and peremptorily ask the male volunteers to leave. If they refused, they were dragged out and pushed on to the road. The assaulted volunteers would return to picket, and then would begin the lathi charges.

Huge crowds would assemble in the evenings to watch our picketing, while mounted police would try to chase them away. On coming to know of my activities, friends such as Manjubhashini, Ammu Swaminadhan, Margaret Cousins and Mrs Reddy would come and express solidarity. Congress leaders and sympathizers brought us coffee and tiffin. Those satyagrahis who were injured in lathi charges were taken for first aid to a building which the Congress had rented for this purpose in the Flower Bazaar[211] area. This had a couple of beds, a doctor and two nurses on duty[212]. I conducted picketing for around 10 days in this fashion, assisted by several male volunteers. The police routinely arrested them and took them away. But I was left to continue freely.

A few days later, following talks between Gandhiji and Lord Irwin[213], a pact was reached, and all those arrested were released. My friends in Vellore prison went back home. I was then at peace with myself and returned to my parents' home. We held a grand reception in honour of Durgabai, who had conducted the Salt Satyagraha in the city.

---

[211] An area in North Madras which, as the name suggests, was where a flourishing wholesale flower market would come up each morning until it was forcibly evicted in the early twenty-first century. A statue of King George V watches over the area even now and the police station is known as the Flower Bazaar Police Station.

[212] Known informally as the Satyagraha Hospital, it was managed by Dr U. Rama Rau (1874–1952), President of the Madras Legislative Council and Founder President of the Music Academy.

[213] Lord Irwin, later the Marquess of Halifax (1881–1959), was Viceroy of India between 1926 and 1931. Gandhi-Irwin Bridge in Egmore commemorates this pact.

Brave Arya

We resumed our swadeshi activities. Ten days before Deepavali, we would begin selling swadeshi items such as khaddar clothes and hand-spun sarees all over the city. In Mylapore, we would stand outside Sampoorna Sastriar & Sons and prevent shoppers from going in to buy silk sarees. They would have to purchase our wares instead. At that time, (Arya) K. Bhashyam[214], a volunteer, came to our assistance and maintained accounts. We sold around Rs 400 to Rs 500 worth of goods each day. A graduate, he was the nephew of N. Gopalaswami Iyengar[215], former railway minister. He had been involved in the nationalist cause since 1920, and having been active in the Civil Disobedience Movement faced enormous difficulties. The police branded him a revolutionary and shadowed him to see if an arrest could be made. He, on the contrary, gave them the slip by travelling from town to town in hay carts and carried on with the nationalist propaganda. While in Madras, one night he climbed the flagstaff at Fort St. George and having removed the Union Jack from it, unfurled the tricolour there[216]! He was the only one in the whole of India to perform this daring feat. He was a talented artist, and the paintings he did of Gandhi

---

[214] Arya K. Bhashyam (1907–99) was a freedom fighter.
[215] Sir N. Gopalaswami Iyengar (1882–1953) was from the Madras Civil Service. Later, he became the dewan of Kashmir, and still later, union minister. Gopalapuram in Chennai commemorates him.
[216] This was on 26 January 1932.

and Bharati can be seen all over the country.

I would also like to remember some other comrades. Krithivas was from Needamangalam. At the age of 16, he gave up his studies at Pachayappa's College and became completely involved in the freedom movement. He was sent to prison for his participation in the Nagpur Flag Satyagraha[217]. Lodged at Amaravati, he became seriously ill and had to be released. Others such as S. Ramanathan[218], Ranganatha Swamigal, and S.D.S. Yogi[219] performed satyagraha at places such as Mannargudi, Thanjavur, Erode, and went to prison. They hardly had any money, yet would hesitate to avail of relatives' hospitality who were wary of housing revolutionaries. So, these men would eat on credit at hotels. There were several others worthy of note. Some were hit senseless by lathis, others bled profusely and struggled to survive. Some were kicked by charging horses and others pressed under boots. They all stand before my eyes now. I can recall Ignatius, Venkatarama Sastry, O.P. Ramaswami,

---

[217] The Flag Satyagraha, which involved freedom fighters demanding the right to hoist the tricolour flag, took place around Nagpur and Jabalpur in 1923.

[218] S. Ramanathan (1895–1970) was a freedom fighter who had a tenuous relationship with the Congress on issues concerning caste, which led him to found the Self Respect Movement, though he later rejoined the Congress and served as a minister in the Rajaji government of 1937.

[219] S.D.S. Yogi (1904–63) was a freedom fighter, writer, poet, playwright and film director.

R.R. Dalavai[220], Acharya, Akshamba, H.D. Raja[221] and the present Communist leader P. Ramamurthy[222]. To fund our activities, we staged plays and conducted exhibitions. S.G. Kittappa[223] and K.B. Sundarambal[224] performed their *Valli Thirumanam* for us and this drew huge collections. Similarly, Harindranath Chattopadhyay[225] staged *Ali Baba and the Forty Thieves* and gave the proceeds to us. I don't know if my aunt Janammal and I were brave, but we were heroines in the eyes of our nephews and nieces.

In the midst of all this, my brother and my son went on an overseas trip in summer. My brother's second child was just four months old and we took him with us to Kodaikanal.

---

[220] R.R. Dalavai (1912–?) was a freedom fighter, who shot to fame in 1928 for throwing phosphorous into the chief justice's car and setting it on fire.

[221] H.D. Raja (1904–59) was a freedom fighter, revolutionary, and later, a magnate in insurance.

[222] P. Ramamurthy (1908–87) was the first leader of the Opposition in Madras State post-Independence.

[223] S.G. Kittappa (1906–33) was a great singer and theatre actor.

[224] K.B. Sundarambal (1908–80) was a powerful devotional singer who began life as a theatre artiste and ran her own all-women's troupe. Married to Kittappa and widowed early, she resumed her theatre career and also acted in films, in which she excelled in saintly roles. A close associate of S. Satyamurti, she participated in the freedom movement by singing songs, for which she was praised by Mahatma Gandhi. Later, she became a cinema theatre owner and also a member of the Madras Legislative Council.

[225] Harindranath Chattopadhyay (1898–1990) was remembered chiefly as the younger brother of Sarojini Naidu, and was also a talented author, poet and actor in his own right. He was married to Kamaladevi.

As We Like It

The freedom movement once again gained momentum in 1932. The Salt Satyagraha was over, and now leaders were being arrested for picketing liquor shops, advocating civil disobedience, and championing swadeshi over foreign goods. Section 144 was again imposed on the city, but nobody seemed to care. My friend the police inspector returned to warn me that a warrant for my arrest was imminent. On coming to know of this, that night I secretly packed a pair of khadi sarees, a plate, a cup, a tumbler and a small mattress in a steel trunk. I also added a charkha.

The next morning, Aunt Janammal and I got to know from the Congress headquarters that we would be arrested by the end of the day. We were advised to picket shops selling foreign cloth. Accordingly, we left without informing our relatives. Kamalabai, also ready to go to prison, accompanied us.

Several years earlier, some of us Swayamsevikas had had gone to meet Gandhiji. An old woman among us asked him how correct it was for him to advise women who were weak as a sex to court arrest. What if the police molested them? To this, Gandhiji replied that it was impossible that women born in the land of Sita and Draupadi could be afraid of the police. 'A chaste woman is like fire,' he replied. 'If she remains firm, no harm can befall her. Women of honour will know how to defend themselves. They may sacrifice their lives but never their self-respect.'

That reply of Gandhiji gave me courage when arrest was imminent. The three of us went to Rattan Bazaar and began picketing outside a shop. Friends brought coffee and refreshments at 3.00 p.m. Within a short while, the mounted police arrived and the sergeant, having got off his horse, showed me the warrant for my arrest. The shopkeeper emerged and asked for my pardon. Janammal, Kamala and I followed the sergeant. The mounted police flanked us as we walked. We were asked to get into a police lorry that stood at a short distance. We sang the songs of Bharati as we were taken to the police station.

We were shifted to the lock-up at 6.00 p.m. Overjoyed at the fulfilment of my desire to go to prison, I went in happily. My parents got to know of what had happened, and came to see me with a packed dinner. My father did not speak to me—in his view, my courting arrest was a futile exercise. My mother said that if I expressed a proper apology, I could be released at once. Had I done all this picketing for the sake a mere pardon? I refused her offer. Janammal was equally firm. We were retained in the lock-up for two days and Kasturi, our cook, brought us coffee, tiffin and meals from home.

Our case came up before Mr Abbas Ali in the Third Metropolitan Magistrate's Court on the third day at 3.00 p.m. V.K. Thiruvenkatachari and my brother Parthasarathy appeared and argued for us. The public prosecutor read out the charge against us—we had picketed the

Chellaram showroom[226]. The sergeant gave evidence. The magistrate asked us if we had broken the law of our own volition. We said we had acted as per Gandhian principles, so did not consider ourselves guilty.

The court, however, did not accept our response and declared us guilty. We were sentenced to six months' simple imprisonment and a fine of Rs 250 each. In the event of a default in payment, our sentence would be extended by two months. Kamalabai was sentenced to simple imprisonment without a fine. As we came from a well-known family, Janammal and I were sentenced to A-category cells, while Kamalabai qualified for a B-category cell.

That night, the three of us were taken to Vellore under escort of women police constables, a sergeant and two jawans, by the Nilgiri Express in a separate compartment. Three miles from Vellore was Thorappadi which had separate prisons for men and women. Even though I was being taken to prison, I felt I was entering a new social world.

At 12 midnight, we got down at Vellore and were transported in a police lorry to the women's prison at Thorappadi. As soon as the two massive steel doors swung open, two Eurasian women emerged and took charge of us. I felt immensely pleased that women of that community were welcoming us who had been charged with waging war against the British government. Our

---

[226] A prominent garments retail showroom of the city.

luggage was kept in the office room, while we were locked up in another room. The door was opened at 6.00 a.m. next morning.

My Prison Experience

As it was forbidden for us to keep jewellery, glass objects, knives and ropes with us, we had taken off all jewellery pieces except the mangalsutra[227] and handed these over to our relatives in the court in Madras. That morning, our luggage was thoroughly searched and we were sent to our cells.

Since there were no separate prisons for political detainees, this was a place where murderers and thieves who had been sentenced to life imprisonment under maximum security were also housed, but they were in a separate block. Political prisoners were divided into A, B and C categories, of which the first two were in a common block, and the third was housed elsewhere. The arrangements were such that prisoners could not meet those in other categories.

Those in category A were allowed to write letters and meet outsiders twice a month. We were also permitted to purchase food worth Rs 25 a month. B-category prisoners could write letters and meet people once a month. Those in category C could do these things only once in three

---

[227] A chain worn by a woman around her neck as a symbol of her wedded status.

months. A- and B-category prisoners were given a pint of milk, a spoonful of coffee powder and some sugar each morning. For lunch, we had sambar rice and curry. In the evening, we had a pint of milk, and at night, sambar rice again.

We were received with love by the women who had been imprisoned before us for their political activities. They informed us that they were given the same food offered to hardened criminals and convicts, and that this was prepared by the prisoners themselves. They had, therefore, preferred to starve rather than eat what was offered, and had not eaten for a week. When prison superintendent Khan came on his rounds the next day, we brought these complaints to his notice and obtained permission to prepare food for everyone ourselves. We were supplied with large clay vessels and wooden ladles. A Brahmin woman, sentenced to life for murder, was assigned to us for cleaning the vessels and fetching water.

Every day, at least five women satyagrahis were brought to the prison. Soon, there were at least a hundred of us and we were a mix of Tamil, Andhra and Malayali women. That integrated family is still fresh before my eyes. The food prepared by the Andhra women was too spicy and did not agree with us. We, therefore, separated the kitchen—they prepared their food on their own, while the Tamil and Malayali women cooked together. We had a rota for the kitchen and we took charge in batches of four on a daily basis.

Janammal and I would go to the matron's room every

morning to collect the food rations. She would give us the allotted quantity for all the Tamil and Malayali women. The rice was as though it had just been harvested[228]. The firewood was damp and as for the vegetables, we had nothing to cut them with and they were of poor quality. As milk and sugar were always insufficient, we had to supplement these by using the monthly Rs 25 that our families deposited for us.

While we were in prison, women from Andhra such as Konda Kanakamma[229], Parvathi Amma[230], V.V. Giri's sister Mahalakshmi[231], Mrs Ranga[232], Dr Thayamma, Rajaji's sister's daughter M.S. Kamala Krishnaswami, Trichy M.S. Padma Ramaswami, Coimbatore Kamala Subri[233], Trichy Kalyani Sastri, Tiruppur Padmavati Asher[234], Madurai Mrs N.M.R. Subbaraman[235], Mrs S.K. SundararamaIyer,

---

[228] New rice did not cook well and it was considered infra dig to eat it.
[229] Ponaka Kanakamma, daughter of Marupuru Konda Reddy (hence, Ambujammal wrote of her as Konda Kanakamma, 1892–1963), was a freedom fighter, writer and social activist.
[230] Muthukulam Parvathi Ammal (1904–74) was a poet, scholar, writer, social reformer and patriot.
[231] Adruti Lakshmibai was Member of the Indian Legislature before Independence and Speaker of Odisha Assembly from 1946 to 1952.
[232] Bharathi Devi was the wife of Prof. N.G. Ranga and a peasants' rights activist.
[233] Kamala Subri (1911–93) was the wife of freedom fighter and composer, Kovai Subri.
[234] Padmavathi Asher was the wife of a mill owner in Coimbatore, and a Congress member.
[235] Parvatavardhini was the wife of 'Madurai Gandhi' N.M.R. Subbaraman (1905–83). Both husband and wife were patriots and

Madurai Thayaramma, and women from Kerala such as Kuttiammaluamma[236], Kathyayani Amma, Matilda, Salem Kamakshi Ammal[237], Rukmini Lakshmipathi, Kothainayaki Ammal, Sivabhogam, and Dr Sakuntala were arrested and brought here.

A week after we were imprisoned, my parents made a surprise visit. As they had come with Mrs V.T. Rangaswami Iyengar[238], who was an honorary Inspectress of Prisons, they were allowed right in. They did not speak to us but my father, on coming to know that we were finding it difficult to cook in mud vessels, later sent us some zinc-lined metal equivalents.

Saturday was when relatives were allowed to meet us. My parents and brother came to see me but when my father discovered that the conversation would have to be via a grille, he flew into a rage. Declaring that he had no wish to converse with his daughter as though she was a caged tiger at a zoo, he left without seeing me. From the next week, we were allowed face-to-face meetings with sufficient distance between us, under the watch of policemen. Every week, my brother came to see me with his wife and children. He brought biscuits, coffee powder, rasam powder and pickles, which I shared with the others.

---

imprisoned. He served as a member of Parliament in the 1960s.

[236] Anakkara Vadakathu Kuttiammalu Ammal (1905–85) was a freedom fighter and a social worker.

[237] Salem Kamakshi Ammal was a freedom fighter and a staunch supporter and member of the Women's Indian Association.

[238] Wife of a prominent lawyer of Madras.

To truly appreciate freedom, a stint in prison is enough. Our day began as per Gandhian principles, with a prayer for the country's welfare. Our singing in chorus could be heard outside the prison walls, and the matron objected to it. But we did not pay any heed to her and continued to pray loudly morning and evening. I was used to bathing only in hot water but while in prison, I learnt how to make do with tap water. Prisoners of A category had a cell to themselves, while those in B category were placed two to a cell. The doors to the cells had grilles and afforded no privacy. When we needed to change our clothes, we had to cover the doors with a cloth. Urinating at night was a major challenge. Our cell doors remained open from 6.00 a.m. to 6.00 p.m. When it came to lock-up time, the matron Julie would course down the corridors, carrying an enormous bunch of keys. Her approach was most intimidating. She would ask each of us to go into our cell and then lock every door. We had to remain inside the whole night. We troubled her quite a bit as she went about her duties and she became quite irritated. But we did not worry about that.

Tuesdays was when inspection happened and Superintendent Khan arrived at 7.30 a.m. for it. We were all given metal tokens bearing our serial number and we were expected to wear it around the neck when inspections happened. But we responded that the mangalsutras our husbands had tied around our necks were sufficient, and that we did not need a mangalsutra from prison! We, therefore, carried our tokens in our hands.

Activities in Prison

Spending time constructively in prison was not a problem. After completing our routine tasks, we engaged ourselves in learning Hindi, embroidery and tailoring. We also made cloth purses that were sold by the prison. I would have a glass of soda every day while at home. During the six months in prison, I did not have it even once, neither did I miss it.

New prisoners came in every day. At the same time, those who had completed their term left, and for these women, we organized farewell feasts. They felt sorry to be leaving us, and at the same time, they looked forward to freedom. We too felt the same. Though we were all women from diverse backgrounds, we became very united and lived together in love and affection. On the days when letters were delivered, prisoners became restless. Reading letters from our relatives kindled emotions in us; some women wept. But I never felt that way. I was very happy while in prison.

On being arrested, I was assailed by doubts as to whether I could ever return to my parental home. After all, I had left without obtaining my father's permission. I was afraid he would refuse me permission to return. I decided that in the event of such an outcome, I would go to Gandhiji's ashram in Wardha. But when I saw him come to prison within a few days of my arrest, and the love and affection with which he made arrangements for my comfort, I came to appreciate his broadness of vision.

To some extent, I also lost the fear I had of my father.

While we were in the women's prison, our male counterparts were lodged in prisons elsewhere. Rajaji, Muthuranga Mudaliar, Bhaktavatsalam and K. Bhashyam were in Vellore prison. This was when Rajaji's eldest son-in-law passed away in Rangoon. He was granted parole to attend the funeral but he refused. We were all very sad when we got the news of his death.

We had some pregnant women among us and they delivered while in prison. We thus had the opportunity to extend the scope of our services. We waited on the mothers, night and day, just as their immediate relatives would have done at home. That way, these women did not miss their families. We took great care of the babies as well. The mothers became very happy and because of that, joy permeated all of us and we forgot we were in prison.

Once we were locked up for the night, we felt very secure as we thought nobody could enter our prison. But despite all of this, when a marauder made his entry, we were panic-stricken. There was pandemonium in the prison, and hearing our screams, the matron rushed in to investigate. But none of us was in a position to explain coherently. One woman pointed to the roof which was shrouded in darkness. Another became more afraid and screamed. The matron could make no sense of what we said, and returned to her quarters. Her departure made us even more frightened. We began screaming all the more. The matron returned an hour later, and having reassured us, once again investigated the reason for all the commotion. We remained incoherent and kept pointing at a corner of the wall. She shone a hurricane lamp on the spot and discovered the root cause of all the trouble—a *jalamandali* spider! She squashed it and left, asking us to sleep in peace. But it took a long while for us to regain our composure. We made fun of each other, asking if we, who were terrified of an insect, could wage war against the British Empire!

Freedom and Fond Farewells

19 July 1932! Janammal, Kamalabai and I were freed at 9.00 a.m. on the completion of our sentence. Despite this, the matron and other officials found it difficult to send us home. Contrary to their expectations, we were not happy leaving the prison, and considered the resumption of domestic life to be a fresh imprisonment. Kothainayaki, Sakuntala Bai and Sivabhogam consoled us and convinced us to leave. Their sentences ran for a year as opposed to our six months, and not wanting to leave them, we kept wandering around the premises. The previous night, a grand farewell had been organized for us by the other inmates.

It was the practice of the inmates to inform their relatives by letter about the date of release, so that someone would be present to take them home. We, on the contrary, did not inform anyone. I, therefore, expected to be received by some Congress volunteer and not by a family member.

The prison doors opened at nine sharp, and the three of us emerged. My brother was waiting in his car. He said that my father had asked me to come home and go nowhere else. The three of us got in with our bags. On seeing me, Father expressed his satisfaction on my safe return. My mother was her equanimous self and spoke as though nothing had happened.

Father's Advice

Within a few days, we resumed our activities of khaddar sales, organizing Congress meetings and welcoming leaders. Though I had been involved with the party thus far, I had never attended the All India Congress Session. My colleagues Krishnabai Nimbkar, Kothainayaki and Manjubhashini were going to the Karachi session. I was very keen to join, but my father refused permission. Then one day, he advised me thus: 'You wanted to go to prison and achieved that goal. Many Congress leaders repeatedly go to prison for the sake of name, fame and garlands. You should not be one of them. Many people will goad you to once again seek imprisonment but you should not give in. Freedom is not attained only by going to prison. All this is meaningless. You are however most free to perform whatever social service you can. That is best suited for you.' He also added: 'I have no objection to your contributing to Gandhi's constructive schemes. I am happy to see you involved in social service.'

What could I say? At that time, I felt what he had said

was reasonable. But I did not have the courage to tell him that I had not gone to prison for the sake of name, fame or garlands. He was well-versed in politics. What experience did I have of the world? I, therefore, had to accept his point of view. I also got to know that my term in prison had caused him considerable stress, leading to an ulcer that lasted three months. I was not informed of this till my return, as he knew I would break down. I, therefore, promised him I would not court imprisonment without his permission.

Over time, satyagraha seemed to have lost momentum. Exactly as Father had predicted, many leaders and comrades goaded me to court imprisonment once more. The Andhra Pradesh Congress Committee had decided to send Margaret Cousins to prison and obtained her consent as well. She asked me if I wanted to accompany her. I said that I could not do so without my father's consent, and that I also felt going to prison was unnecessary. She went ahead and was sentenced to a year.

The Birds Take Wing

I consider 1934 to be a significant year in my life. That was when several women who worked alongside me parted and went their individual ways. The Women's Swadeshi League also suspended its activities. Krishnabai married Dr Nimbkar and went away to study medicine. Kameswari Ammal returned to her native Andhra. Sivabhogam became the first woman to qualify as an auditor and apprenticed herself with the firm Sastry & Shah. Kamalabai came from an indigent family, so Janammal and I funded her going to Allahabad to learn Hindi. She finished that course in a year, and on her return, joined the Hindi Prachar Sabha as a teacher. Kothainayaki resumed publishing her magazine *Jaganmohini*. Katyayani worked at a khaddar depot in Thiruvananthapuram. She quit that job and came to Madras to study law. Having finished a year, she went back to Thiruvananthapuram, completed her BL there, and set up practice as a lawyer. In this way, each one built a life for herself. Though we had parted, we remained in touch through correspondence.

Ever since my return, I had been restless. How much of yarn could one spin? How long could one study Hindi? Congress activities had also practically ceased. I found household activities tedious. After all, I had abandoned them all and gone to prison! These days, women from affluent households often say they are bored. That word was not current in my time, but I felt I was leading a useless life.

Since joining the Congress, I had maintained correspondence with Gandhiji. I would often seek clarifications for my doubts and act according to his advice. This gave me some peace. I wrote to him seeking permission to spend a few days at his Wardha Ashram and be involved in its activities. He replied stating that he was soon going to be in Bombay and asked me to meet him there. I made preparations for my journey.

Election Campaign

Readers will recall that when C.R. Das set up the Swaraj Party within the Congress to fight the elections, there were some no-changers who had objected. C. Rajagopalachari was among the leaders of the latter group. He had set up an ashram at Tiruchengode where he espoused Gandhian principles, such as spinning khadi and eradicating untouchability. The same Rajaji had a change of mind in 1934, and supported the entry of the Congress into electoral politics. The party fielded Lakshmi Sankaran as its candidate for Kallidaikurichi. She was opposed by Sankaran Pillai of the Justice Party. Lakshmi Sankaran invited all her erstwhile prison comrades to campaign for her. Acceding to her request, Rukmini Lakshmipathi, Kothainayaki, Kalyani Sastry, Janammal, Salem Kamakshi Ammal, Gomathi Sarma, Kamalabai and I went to Tirunelveli.

We organized meetings and campaigned at places such as Sri Vaikuntham, Tiruchendur, Alwarthirunagari, Nanguneri, Seithinganallur, and also in parts of the Tirunelveli constituency, such as Veeravanallur, Pathamadai and Sevval. We had been given a ramshackle bus to travel in. We also used this opportunity to visit the famed temples in the Tirunelveli area. One day, we went to Tiruchendur, had *darshan* of Murugan and bathed in the sea. We did not feel like leaving the place. We also bathed at the waterfalls in Papanasam and Thirukutralam. We bathed in the Tamraparni River practically every day.

Was that all? We feasted on the temple offerings such as tamarind rice, curd rice, *sundal* and *vadai*. And we were invited to several prominent households where we ate dishes such as *chakkaprathaman*, milk *payasam*, plantain chips and avial.

Campaigning apart, these visits to temples, the baths in the river, and the lunches all raised our spirits. My depression vanished. On the last day of our campaign, we were scheduled to visit Sevval near Pathamadai. Our bus was stopped by the police before the bridge leading to the village. We were informed that the Opposition had assembled a crowd armed with sticks to attack us, and that they were waiting for us on the other side of the bridge. Fearing violence, the police did not permit us to proceed.

Despite their entreaties, we were firm in our resolve to proceed. Some of our fellow campaigners decided to take up the matter with the police commissioner and left. No matter what we said, the police did not permit us to go ahead. An argument broke out and matters continued this way till 10 p.m. We then got information that the crowd that had assembled to hear us had dispersed owing to the delay. There was nothing to do but return.

The ceaseless travel for 10 days and the lack of proper sleep affected my health. I fell ill with pneumonia. My temperature rose to 104 degrees and I was delirious. The fever did not abate the next day, so my father was informed by telegram. Janammal and I were sent by train to Madras, with a doctor in attendance. The others left for Thiruvananthapuram. An ambulance awaited me at Egmore Station, and I was brought home in it. I knew nothing of all these happenings. Under Dr Sitapati's care, I recovered within a couple of days.

I Attend the Bombay Congress

When Gandhiji first stayed at our house, my father introduced my mother and me to him. Gandhiji asked my mother what my name was. She explained that I was named Ambujavalli after my grandmother, and that everyone referred to me as Pappamma. To this, Gandhiji responded that Ambujavalli seemed a very long name, so he would call me Ambujam. From then on, whenever he met my father, he would ask him how Ambujam was doing. I then got to know that he had included me in his list of adopted daughters. Those who lived in the ashram addressed Gandhiji as Bapu (Father) and Kasturba as Ba (Mother). When I corresponded with Gandhiji, I always addressed him as Bapu.

I decided to honour his invitation and attend the Bombay Congress. Rail reservations were made for Janammal, Kothainayaki and me. This time, I was able to convince my father to permit me to go. My brother's wife delivered a child on the day of my departure, so I postponed my departure by two days. I eventually left for Bombay, with my uncle Venuswami as my escort.

The Bombay Congress, held under the presidentship

of Rajendra Prasad[239], was a grand event. A huge *pandal* had been erected on the Worli sea face, and the venue was reached after crossing six gates. It was rumoured that Subhas Chandra Bose was bringing a huge group of people to disrupt the proceedings, so there was tight security[240]. Each morning, I would cross the six gates and reach Gandhiji's camp. I stayed with him the whole day and returned to my place of stay only in the evening. Gandhiji had come to the Congress session at the request of Rajendra Prasad, but he did not participate much in the proceedings. Unless called for, he did not leave his camp.

I saw leaders walking in to consult him, exuding confidence and even arrogance in their stride. But his mischievous glance, his mocking smile, and a few but sharp observations soon put them in their place. I would be fanning him, and he made fun of me saying I had come all the way to swat flies. To this, I replied that I was prepared to do any task at his bidding.

Most of all, I liked being in his presence and listening to him, and did not consider attending the Congress session to be of much consequence.

---

[239] Babu Rajendra Prasad (1884–1963) was a freedom fighter and the first president of India.
[240] By then, relations between Bose on one side and the Gandhi-Nehru faction on the other had soured considerably.

A Successful Hunger Strike

At the end of the Bombay session, when I went to take leave of Gandhiji, he asked me if I could come to the ashram on 1 November. I promised him I would and returned to Madras. I had given him that assurance without thinking of the consequences. His invitation seemed to me to have been issued more as a challenge, and I had accepted it.

There was just one week for my departure to Wardha when I broached the subject gently with my father. He flared up at once. 'You cannot go there!' he shouted. 'It will not be conducive to your health. It was a big mistake to have sent you to the Bombay Congress!'

I pleaded with him. I requested my mother to intercede. But nothing seemed to work.

What was to be done? I had promised Gandhiji, so I had to go. I, therefore, came to a conclusion. I remembered Gandhiji's principle of going on hunger strikes. I decided I would embark on one to change my father's mind.

Hunger strike is an excellent but very intricate tool to take up. Gandhiji himself had often spoken of how and when this was to be taken up—that is, if someone did not accept our point of view, we could embark on a hunger strike to get them to change their mind! But this would work only with people who have unbounded love for us. And our point of view had to be reasonable as well, and we had to firmly believe in it. Only if all these conditions were met would a hunger strike be effective.

Accordingly, with a view of changing my parents' minds, I announced that I was giving up food until I was permitted to go to Wardha. I went and lay down in my room. For three days, I had nothing except water. Why, I even gave up coffee. It was somewhat difficult on day one, but from the second day, I got used to remaining hungry. On learning of my fast, my relatives, friends, comrades and acquaintances came home to convince me to give it up. My son, who was then studying for his BA, and my brother Parthasarathy too joined the chorus. Even my mother tried. But I did not give up. My fast continued.

On the afternoon of the third day, my son brought a telegram from Gandhiji. In it, he had messaged that he had come to know of my fast, and of the worry it was causing my parents. He asked me to give it up at once. He instructed me to convince my parents that my desire to go to Wardha was a perfectly reasonable one, and that by my going there, no harm would come to me. On the contrary, it would benefit me. Having obtained their permission, I was to come to Wardha.

Gandhiji had come to know of my hunger strike by means of a telegram that Harihara Sarma, the Secretary of the Hindi Prachar Sabha[241], had sent him after he had seen me.

---

[241]The Dakshin Bharat Hindi Prachar Sabha—an organization established in Madras by Gandhiji to propagate Hindi in the southern part of India.

Despite Gandhiji's message, I did not give up my fast. The next morning, my father came to see me and said he would himself take me to Wardha in a couple of days. I then broke my fast. True to his words, he personally escorted me to Wardha in the first week of November. He had left the Congress some years earlier. His differences of opinion with Gandhiji continued, yet he undertook this journey for my sake.

Life in the Ashram

I still can't forget the way tears streamed down my father's face when he left me with Gandhiji and took leave. That was the day when Gandhiji and I understood the love my father had for me.

Gandhiji consoled my father, 'Don't worry. Your Ambujam can stay a few days with us. I will take good care of her. I have several foster daughters and I consider her to be one. She will never conduct herself in a manner that will cause you distress. Please convey this to your wife as well. She will remain a true daughter to you both.' On hearing Gandhiji's words, my father, for the sake of the outside world, acted as though he was reassured. But I did not believe this was so!

Gandhiji displayed the same interest he had in politics in matters concerning the welfare of his friends' families. He never allowed differences of view in political matters affect personal relationships. The affection he showered on me was chiefly on account of my being his friend's daughter. He had himself explained this to me several times. He passed all the fruits he received to me. I once came to know that I had unknowingly consumed all the honey meant for him. I deeply regretted this. He observed that I wrote lying prone and got Sri Jamnalal Bajaj[242] to make a special sloping desk for me. From this, you can know how deeply he cared for me.

When he sent for me, I was deeply apprehensive that he was calling to chide me for some gaffe I had committed in my ignorance. I rushed up the stairs and reached his presence completely out of breath. He laughingly said, 'Ambujam, I have got this desk especially made for you. You cannot lie down and write anymore!' I was wonderstruck. Thereafter I lost all my fear of him; my love for him increased manifold.

I had mentioned that it was bitterly cold when I went to Wardha. It was November after all. Gandhiji, Kasturba, Mirabehn, Abdussalam[243] and others lived in the upper floor of a bungalow, in the garden of the ladies' wing of the ashram. Vinoba Bhave[244] and others stayed on the ground floor. One rainy afternoon, some days after my arrival, a few ladies and I were huddled together in

---

[242]Seth Jamnalal Bajaj (1889–1942) was an industrialist and a close associate of Mahatma Gandhi. He founded the Bajaj Group of Companies.

[243]Ambujammal clearly meant Bibi Amtus Salam (d. 1985), a close woman associate of Mahatma Gandhi.

[244]Acharya Vinobha Bhave (1895–1982) was a Gandhian who was the leader of the Bhoodan Movement, wherein people voluntarily gifted land to be distributed among the landless.

the veranda, even as a series of visitors met Gandhiji in the inner hall.

I had been allergic to rain from childhood and would instantly catch a cold. Consequently, my father never allowed me to step out in the rain. In order to prevent my feet from coming in contact with the wet earth, my father had ensured that the area surrounding our house was cemented over.

The gathering darkness, rain and the cold, combined with thought of slush all around the Wardha Ashram, depressed me. I was racked with a longing for home and my parents. I was homesick and in tears.

Suddenly I heard Bapu's voice: 'Leelavati[245]! Ambujam! What are you doing in the rain?'

He took us inside to where Kasturba, Prabhavati[246], Mirabehn and Amtus Salam were. There, in the light of the hurricane lamp, we began reading and also spinning the charkha. In contrast to the dampness and rain outside, the warmth in this room was so comforting. My fears vanished—that cold night passed in comfort.

Janammal came to the ashram a fortnight or so after me. We stayed with the Mahatma. Our day began at 4.00 a.m. when a bell rang. Another bell at 4.30 a.m. summoned us to prayer. This took place in dim lamplight

---

[245]Leelavati Munshi (1899–1978) was a member of the Congress, and a child widow who later married K.M. Munshi, famed lawyer, governor and union minister. She was a writer and a legislator.

[246]Prabhavati Devi (1906–73) was the wife of the socialist leader Jayaprakash Narayan, and an ardent follower of Mahatma Gandhi.

in the bitter cold, in an open space on the upper storey where the Mahatma stayed. In absolute peace and quiet, this prayer lasted for half an hour and we attended, wrapped in blankets from head to foot. Thereafter, we observed silence for a while.

As soon as the Mahatma got up to leave, we too dispersed to perform the ashram duties. A large glass of milk was served at 7.00 a.m. It was compulsory for everyone to take up some task or the other. Bapu was involved in everything—from routine tasks to great matters of the state. Besides this, he also took it upon himself to care for the sick, cheer them up and encourage them to work. His toothless smile gave solace and his compassionate glance filled us with courage.

The food at the ashram comprised some rice, tough rotis, lentils, a lightly salted curry and curd. Janammal could not adjust to this food and was granted special permission to prepare Madras rasam for herself. The ashram fare disagreed with me too, but Gandhiji asked me to eat uncooked food instead. This was one of his many experiments in the food area.

Fresh milk was kept in a vessel immersed in cold water to prevent curdling. I had this and also apples, oranges and sweet lime. Honey was a substitute for sugar, and I had salted carrot, cabbage, radish, tomatoes, and spinach with a dash of lemon. Raw fruits and vegetables were washed in a solution of potassium permanganate, and then washed in clear water. I had to chew these well when I ate. Besides, I also had curd prepared by milk mixed with lime juice and kept in sunlight.

This diet did me no harm, but no matter how much I ate, I never felt as satisfied as I did when I ate the rice of South India. Like everything else, I discussed this with Bapu and he instructed me to drink milk whenever I felt hungry. On my return to Madras, I found this diet disagreed with me, and I reverted to my usual eating habits.

When I was thus following the ashram regime, it was time for the festival of Deepavali and my mother sent a parcel of eatables. This was opened in Bapu's presence and found to contain *burfi*, *murukku* and *cheedai*. 'On seeing this, I am sure you must be salivating,' mocked Gandhiji. 'After all, your mother has prepared all this with love and affection.' To this, I replied, 'Bapuji, I don't need any of this.' He then instructed me to distribute them among the ashram children. Later, he enquired from Prabhavati if I really did not even taste what was sent. On coming to know that I had remained true to my word, he praised me for learning to control my craving for traditional foods.

Janammal and I participated in ashram duties to the extent possible. We were unused to drawing water from the well, washing our clothes and scouring vessels, and there not being much time to spare, we could do but little. Devdas Gandhi[247] sang the *Tulsi Ramayana*[248]

---

[247] Devdas Gandhi (1900–57) was the youngest son of Mahatma Gandhi and Kasturba.

[248] *Ramcharitmanas*—the Ramayana in the Awadhi dialect was composed by the sixteenth-century Bhakti poet Goswami Tulsidas.

strumming a tambura (tanpura) to maintain the pitch. We joined in even as the Mahatma murmured the lyrics. I can still recall the sweetness of the song, the melody of the harmonium, and the voices of the ashram women singing in chorus. At 12 noon, we would spin the charkha for half an hour. These two activities filled our minds with a great sense of peace.

We would go out in the evenings. We collected pebbles as we went along and brought them back to the ashram to lay a road. Even Bapu was not spared this task. It was fun to watch him bend and pick pebbles as he walked.

Janammal and I did not think even once of home for the two-and-a-half months we stayed in the ashram. In some ways, life in prison and life in the ashram were not different. But the peace, satisfaction, courage and clarity of thought we experienced in the ashram could never be obtained elsewhere. As long as I stayed in the ashram, I felt like a daughter staying under the care of a loving father.

I Return Home

I came back home in January 1935. The stay at the ashram had taught me a few lessons. I greatly desired to involve myself in social service. My son Krishnaswami had joined the Indian Bank in Bangalore, and I too went there. It was my lot to care for my family, so I did not then involve myself in any public activities. The next year, my son relocated to Madras on account of ill health. He was married to Padma, the eldest daughter of R. Srinivasa Iyengar, an income tax officer in Bombay. The wedding took place in Madras. Even though we were from the groom's side, my father took care of all arrangements. After his wedding, my son was transferred to Bombay.

Around this time, Bihar and Quetta were rocked by earthquakes. Gandhiji instructed Janammal and me by letter to collect funds for the Bihar earthquake victims. We put together a band of volunteers and collected a small amount. Between 1934 and 1936, Gandhiji embarked on a Harijan Yatra to eradicate untouchability.

In order to teach Hindi to the people of South India, Gandhiji had sent Devdas Gandhi to Madras in 1921. The Dakshin Bharat Hindi Prachar Sabha was begun in T. Nagar, under the leadership of Rajaji; Harihara Sarma was its secretary. He and his wife Gomati had spent several years with Gandhiji at the Sabarmati Ashram. Ramnath Goenka[249] was its treasurer and Nageswara Rao Pantulu[250] a committee member. I too served as a committee member. Hindi teachers undertook home tuitions as well, so Janammal and I learnt Hindi from Sivarama Sarma.

---

[249]Ramnath Goenka (1904–91) was the founder of the Indian Express Group of Publications.
[250]Desoddharaka Kasinathuni Nageswara Rao Pantulu (1867–1938) was a freedom fighter, a journalist, and inventor of the Amrutanjan balm. He was also a resident of Luz Church Road.

It was decided that the sabha would send representatives to the Hindi Conference to be held in Delhi.

Badrinath Pilgrimage

Accordingly, Gomati Sarma, Rukmini Lakshmipathi and I left with 15 other women on a tour of North India. My father gave permission, and Uncle Venuswami was sent as an escort. Once the conference concluded in Delhi, we left on a pilgrimage for Haridwar. We stayed at a rest house built by Madhava Teertha, a South Indian sanyasi, and therefore, it was referred to as the Madrasi Shala. A bathing *ghat* with protective railings and proper steps leading to the Ganga was close by. The rest house was part-funded by my father and by the leading business family of V. Perumal Chetty[251]. A South Indian family was stationed here to take care of pilgrims from the South and offer food to them.

Having lunched and rested, we went to the river in the evening. We watched in wonder as people bathed in the swiftly flowing Ganga. In the evening, women floated lamps together with some other articles on leaves. The lamps floating in the water at sunset was a beautiful sight. It was believed by the women that their lamps remaining afloat for long were an augury of a happy married life.

---

[251] V. Perumal Chetty & Sons was a leading business concern of Madras, with interests in stationery and printing.

Having bathed in the river and enjoyed the sights, we boarded a bus and departed for Rishikesh. We bathed there in the Rishikund hot-water spring, and later, in the Ganga. This being the month of March, the weather was pleasant. Bhajan groups and storytellers were performing on the banks of the river. On seeing these, I could catch a glimpse of what ancient India would have been like. That evening, we reached Lakshman Jhoola at six. Here the holy Ganga flowed silently at a great distance below. On our side of the river were monasteries, temples, rest houses and eateries. On the opposite side, we could see the Himalayan foothills and great forests. The human eye could not take in so much beauty. Next to the river ran a four-foot-wide path. This was the route the ancients took to ascend to Badrinath.

We got off our bus, left our luggage at the rest house, and slowly descended the steps to the Ganga. The water was an emerald green, and the lamps from the neighbouring temples reflected in it. To me, it seemed as if gold nuggets were shining on a green carpet. The water was ice cold. How to bathe in it? I overcame all fears and took a dip. It seemed as if I would freeze but that sensation lasted for just a second. I was filled with a new energy. The ringing of bells from the temples indicated that the evening worship was going on, and to us it seemed as if we were in heaven.

Harihara Sarma, Sivarama Sarma, Satyanarayana and Rishikeshji—who accompanied us—lit an earthen oven in which they roasted whole potatoes and made rotis with their bare hands. This is what we ate. We were told that this was the food that all Badrinath pilgrims ate. The next morning, we awoke to the sound of slippers clip-clopping on the road. This was the sign that the pilgrims had begun their ascent to Badrinath. They walked with a staff topped by an upturned pot, two black blankets on their back and a turban on the head. On seeing them walk by in batches, I was gripped by a strong desire to walk with them to Badrinath.

In these North Indian bazaars, there was no dearth of hot milk, curds, puri-halwa and jalebi. They sold milk and curd in earthen pots which we discarded after we had eaten. In our desire to go to Badri, we decided to walk at least for some of the distance with the pilgrims. There was a rope bridge across the Ganga, which was the Lakshman Jhoola. You needed to cross this to continue on your way to Badri. Around 50 miles on this route was the rest house at Garud Chatti. In addition, there were halting places every five miles, constructed by a North Indian philanthropist. It took around a month to walk to Badrinath. Therefore, poor pilgrims were given flour and potatoes free at these rest houses. At the Kali Kambliwala Chattram, they gifted two black blankets to each pilgrim, hence the name Kali (Black) Kambli (Black) Chattram (Rest House). The waterfall at Garud Chatti had a mortar that was operated by the force of the water, and it was a sight to behold. The ancients had harnessed water energy long before scientists came up with hydroelectricity.

It was past 9.00 a.m. when, rather reluctantly, we

returned, even as the other pilgrims marched on, shouting 'Jai!' every now and then. As it was April, there were pilgrims who were mounted on mules, and we could also see mothers with babies securely tied to their backs in baskets, walking along on that narrow pathway with other pilgrims.

We went on to Swargashram and Haridwar and then proceeded to Dehradun, where we inspected the Kanya Gurukul (school for girls) set up by the Arya Samaj. We also visited Mussoorie. We then went to the Kangri Gurukul founded by the Arya Samaj, just four miles from Haridwar. We had been invited to attend the annual convocation of this institution. Around 200 students, ranging between the ages of seven and 10, studied here. On joining, they were anointed with the sacred thread and were trained in chanting the 'Gayatri Mantra' morning and evening, performing fire sacrifices and reciting the Vedas. Classes right up to BA level were in Hindi. Students were required to stay there for seven years without a single visit home. Their parents could come and visit them once every year. The students were known as *snatak*s (graduates).

We were accommodated in a separate building. Each morning, the students got up at 4.30 a.m., performed *sandhyavandanam*[252], and then arranged themselves around a huge sacrificial fire in the main hall and chanted the 'Gayatri Mantra'. Lessons in the Upanishads were

---

[252] Worship of the sun to be performed thrice a day.

imparted thereafter. During the three days we were there, there were several discourses in Hindi.

From there, we went to Lahore via Kanpur. It was then a part of India. There we saw a large prayer hall built by the Arya Samaj, the Shalimar Gardens and the Ravi River. We were delighted at the natural beauty. At that time, there were hardly any taxi or bus facilities. We had to go around in horse carriages, such as the tonga and the *ekka*. As the streets were very narrow, these vehicles rubbed against the steps and platforms of houses on both sides as we rode along.

We then went to the Triveni Sangam in Allahabad. Prominent writers such as Premchand[253], Tripathi[254], Mahadevi Varma[255] and Sundarlal had made arrangements for our stay and hosted dinners for us. We went by boat to bathe at the spot where the Ganga, the Yamuna and the Saraswati merged. Worship was performed while in the boat, and we were given sacred threads, ash, vermilion and other offerings.

We saw the sacred hermitage of Sage Bharadwaja, celebrated in the Puranas, and a huge banyan tree under which it is said the seven sages discussed and discoursed on the Puranas for over a month. From

---

[253] Munshi Premchand (1880–1936) was a celebrated writer. Ambujammal had translated his novel *Bazaar-e-Husn* into Tamil, and this later became *Seva Sadanam*, a Tamil film in 1938, which saw M.S. Subbulakshmi debut as an actor.
[254] Probably Suryakant Tripathi 'Nirala' (1897–1961) the poet.
[255] Mahadevi Varma (1907–1987) was a famed writer and poet.

there we proceeded to Varanasi, where we stayed at the residence of Sundaram, a South Indian who was Secretary to Pandit Madan Mohan Malviya[256] at the Banaras Hindu University. He showed us around the city and Sarnath. The members of the Nagari Pracharini Sabha gave us a grand reception and honoured us.

It was from Sundaram that I got to know that my father had donated Rs 10,000 to the Banaras Hindu University. We then returned to Madras via Calcutta.

We benefitted in another way from this tour—we were praised for the manner in which we spoke in Hindi and the proficiency we had attained in the language!

---

[256] Pandit Madan Mohan Malviya (1861–1946) was four times Congress President, a scholar, and Founder of the Banaras Hindu University.

6

Gandhiji's Failure

I MET GANDHIJI WHEN HE CAME ON HIS HARIJAN YATRA TO Madras. He was staying at the Thakkar Bapa Vidyalaya[257] in Kodambakkam. 'What are your father's views on Congress politics?' he had asked. 'Has his anger cooled a little? It will be good if he returns to the party. Can you not convince him?'

I said it was not easy to change his mind, and that he would definitely not listen to what I said. To this, Gandhiji said he would meet Father in person and try to persuade him. 'Make arrangements for us to meet,' he said. 'Let me see if I succeed where you did not.'

I did what he asked me to and was at least successful in organizing the meeting. I took Gandhiji home by car the next evening at around six. My father and he had extended discussions, but there was no change in my father's views. I was upset that he remained unmoved

---

[257]Named after Amritlal Vithaldas Thakkar, also known as Thakkar Bapa (1869–1951), a prominent social worker and follower of Mahatma Gandhi. Founded in 1933, the school still functions in the premises where Gandhiji laid the foundation stone in 1946.

Gandhiji's Failure 173

despite Gandhiji's personal visit.

I, however, did not feel sad or disappointed for my sake. After all, I knew it was not an easy task to get him to change his views. But because it was a failure for Gandhiji, I felt sad. After his withdrawal from politics, Father remained essentially homebound. He occupied himself with bringing out a fresh edition of Mayne's *Hindu Law*[258]. This took about two years.

Seshasayee[259] of Trichy was a close friend of my father's. My brother Parthasarathy wanted to become an industrialist like him, but my father detested the world of commerce. Therefore, my brother shared chambers at the High Court with V.K. Tiruvenkatachari and practised as a lawyer.

Even though Father had distanced himself from the Congress, leaders such as K. Bhashyam and Satyamurti would keep him abreast of developments, and from time to time, also ascertained his views on events as they unfolded. My father also maintained an active correspondence with Subhas Chandra Bose, and he attended the Tripura Congress session at the express invite of the latter.

In 1936, Sister Subbalakshmi began the Mylapore

---

[258]John D. Mayne's *Hindu Law and Usage*, written first in 1878, remains a seminal work in matters of law. Mayne (1828–1917) was the advocate general of Madras.

[259]Brothers-in-law R. Seshasayee and V. Seshasayee were pioneering industrialists of the Trichy region. The former, who was also a pioneering aviator, died in 1941, and the latter in 1958.

Ladies Club at Padma Vilas, the bungalow where her Sarada Vidyalaya was housed. Mangalammal, the daughter of C. Rajam[260], and I became its secretaries. Janammal, K. Savitri Ammal and Mrs Sitapati were members of the executive committee. Sister Subbalakshmi was the president. Women from the upper echelons of Mylapore society joined the club, and we played games such as badminton and tennis. A year later, the club purchased the property of Janammal's brother Desikachariar, built the premises for itself and shifted there[261]. To fund this, we sought donations and also issued debentures for Rs 300 and Rs 400. I taught Hindi to the members of this club, and the classes with about 30 students took place from 2.00 p.m. to 4.00 p.m.

During these years, Janammal and I continued selling khadi and participating in nationalist meetings.

A Tamil Magazine

The Women's Indian Association was functioning from Pantheon House in Egmore. It was headed by Dr Muthulakshmi Reddy, while its secretary was a Parsi lady. Dr Reddy was bringing out a Tamil monthly titled *Stri Dharma* on behalf of the association. In 1933, owing to space constraints, the WIA shifted to a property owned

---

[260]C. Rajam (1882–1955) was an industrialist and founder of Madras Institute of Technology.
[261]Vidya Mandir Senior Secondary School was founded by the Mylapore Ladies Club on the premises and still functions from there.

by the Zamindar of Jaggampet in Royapettah. At that time, Dr Reddy approached me and asked me to take on the responsibilities of secretary and treasurer of the association. The Mylapore Ladies Club was then headed by Mrs N.V. Raghavan[262], while K. Savitri Ammal and I were the secretaries. Once I took on the responsibilities at the WIA, I planned some new activities there.

Spinning thread and tailoring, teaching Hindi commenced. Dr Sitapati's daughter Savitri Rajan[263] became assistant secretary. Women from Egmore, Mylapore, Thiruvallikeni, Royapettah and Mambalam joined the two organizations and attended classes. P.K. Kalpakam, M. Bhaktavatsalam's daughter Sarojini Varadappan[264], and Vasumathi Ramaswami[265] also joined the Hindi class.

Sales through the WIA

We began a cooperative store under the auspices of the WIA. We purchased pickles, fritters, pappadums and other such items prepared by women from financially weak families and then sold them with a small markup. In this way, many poor women received some income.

---

[262]Wife of N.V. Raghavan (1879–1943), Accountant General of the Greater Indian Peninsular Railway and finance minister of Indore State.
[263]Savitri Rajan (d. 1991) was a social worker and a distinguished musicologist.
[264]Sarojini Varadappan (1921–2013) was a prominent social worker.
[265]Vasumathi Ramaswami (1917–2004) was a social worker and an author.

There was a woman called Janamma, a Vaishnavite widow who lived in the Kusapettai area of Mylapore. She had trained in Ayurveda at the Narayana Ashrama in Kanchipuram. She was an active participant in the protest meetings of the Congress. She came forward to run this cooperative store. The WIA thus took on activities like this and also organized meetings to highlight women's rights.

Dr Reddy, though not a direct participant in the freedom struggle, was greatly devoted to Gandhian ideals and principles. She organized women's meetings where we could highlight the importance of khaddar, eradication of untouchability, and the evils of alcohol. She spoke up strongly at meetings against the British government's lathi charges and mistreatment of political prisoners.

Sir R.K. Shanmukham Chetty[266] was the dewan of Cochin. He invited my father to the inauguration of the High Court in that princely state. Though he and Dr Subbaroyan were Justice Party members[267], they were close friends of my father. I, too, went with my father for this event. We stayed at a very large hotel on Willingdon Island. Sir Alladi Krishnaswami Iyer[268] and Patro too attended the event.

---

[266] Sir R.K. Shanmukham Chetty (1892–1953) was a lawyer, politician, dewan of Cochin and first finance minister of independent India. He was the husband of the distinguished dancer T. Balasaraswati.

[267] As clarified earlier, Dr P. Subbaroyan was not a Justice Party member.

[268] Sir Alladi Krishnaswami Iyer (1883–1953) was a brilliant lawyer who also served as Advocate General, Government of Madras. Later, he was a key member of the Constituent Assembly and a major contributor to the Constitution of India.

After the inauguration, I went to Poonkunnam to meet my friend from prison—the advocate Katyayini. She was a great patriot and a follower of Gandhi in every way. She married N. Ramaswami, who was the secretary of the All Indian Weavers Association, and the two later lived in Thanjavur where they took care of the Sarvodaya publications.

The Gandhi Couple in Madras

In 1937, Gandhiji and Kasturba came to Madras to preside over the convocation of the Hindi Prachar Sabha. Janki Devi Bajaj[269] and Mrs Munshi came with them. I organized a garden party for Kasturba. It was in the same year that, as per the desire of Gandhiji, Rajendra Prasad and Jamnalal Bajaj stayed at Sri Ramanasramam[270] for a few weeks. Satyanarayana, secretary of the Hindi Prachar Sabha, arranged for M.S. Balammal to take care of these two honoured guests at the ashram and drive them around.

Subhas Stays at My House

Subhas Chandra Bose came to Madras in 1938 and met my father at our house. That evening, there was a

---

[269]Janki Devi Bajaj (1893–1956) was the wife of Seth Jamnalal Bajaj, and a freedom fighter.
[270]The hermitage in Tiruvannamalai of Bhagavan Sri Ramana Maharshi (1879–1951).

meeting at the beach, which my father also attended. Subhas had come to Madras with a view to begin a new party opposed to the Congress. He sought my father's assistance, but Father refused to consider the idea. I was so upset when he had not acceded to Gandhiji's invite to re-join the Congress. I was now delighted at his refusal to join Subhas.

World War II

World War II began in 1939. As Britain opposed Germany and Japan, India had to perforce enter the conflict. At that time, Bose was under strict surveillance as the British suspected that he could collude with the Germans. He was placed under house arrest. But after a few days, we received the news that he had vanished and probably fled to Germany. Later, we got to know that he had entered into an agreement with the Japanese to oppose the British, and eventually gain control over India. During those days, my father would forever be listening to the news on the radio. He was greatly saddened on coming to know of Bose going to Japan. Soon, we got to know of the invasion of Singapore.

Indian National Army

After the fall of Singapore to the Japanese, rumours began to circulate that the victors would soon be marching on India with the help of Subhas Chandra Bose. A contingent of the Indian army was then in Singapore. After Subhas allied with the Japanese, many Indians left the British army and joined him. With their help, he formed the Indian National Army (INA)[271] and became its commander. It should be remembered that he collaborated with the Japanese only with a view to defeat the British and make India independent.

The details of the INA's exercises were broadcast throughout India, and many patriots silently left for Singapore to join in the effort. My friend Ammu Swaminadhan's daughter Lakshmi[272] was then working as a doctor in Madras. She resigned from her job and joined the INA in Singapore. Subhas made her captain of the women's wing of the INA. Many young men left the city for Singapore to join the INA. When this news spread, the nation was thrown into turmoil. It could be even said that it cleaved the country in two. Some welcomed the Japanese invasion of India and praised Subhas's courage. Others denounced him as a traitor and said that the Japanese were untrustworthy. They felt that once they had control over India, they would never leave. My father was of the latter view. He kept saying that what Subhas Babu had done was wrong.

---

[271] The INA existed as an entity in Singapore before the arrival of Bose there. He was therefore not its founder but he did become its leader.
[272] Captain Lakshmi (1914–2012) was the younger daughter of Dr S. Swaminadhan and Ammu. She married Prem Sahgal of the INA.

Gandhiji at Sevagram

By this time, the Mahatma had left Wardha and was residing around five miles away at Sevagram. He had issued a call to the youth of the nation to go serve people in the villages. Though he kept reiterating this, those living in the city hesitated, so in order to set an example, he began living in Sevagram.

After the wedding of my son Krishnaswami, I took him and his wife Padma to seek Gandhiji's blessings. This was my first visit to Sevagram. At that time, Aryanayakam[273] and his wife Asha Devi[274] had devised a new scheme of education and were taking pre-school classes for village children. He was from Sri Lanka (formerly known as Ceylon) and highly qualified. Gandhiji was greatly impressed with his new education system. He was of the view that geography, history, science, maths, and other lessons could be made part of the vocational training curriculum.

At this time, Janki Devi Bajaj was running a cow shelter for the benefit of the children in the village and in the ashram.

---

[273] E.R.W. Aryanayakam was private secretary to Rabindranath Tagore.
[274] Asha Devi Aryanayakam (1901–72) was a freedom fighter and an educationist.

J.C. Kumarappa and Bharatan Kumarappa

At that time, J.C. Kumarappa[275] and Bharatan Kumarappa[276], two brothers of the Christian faith, were staying with Gandhiji. Bharatan had established a permanent exhibition of village crafts and was supervising it. The two brothers had studied and qualified abroad. Had they so desired, they could have easily obtained high-level government jobs. But because of their devotion to Gandhiji and their nationalistic fervour, they involved themselves in fulfilling his vision at enormous personal sacrifice.

Kumudini's Wardha Trip

The famed writer Kumudini[277], who belonged to the Srirangam Thathachari family[278], came to see me in June 1940. She met with Aryanayakam and Gandhiji when they had come on a tour of South India, and was told by Aryanayakam that she ought to visit Sevagram at least once. As it was her first visit to Wardha, she requested that I accompany her. I joined her the very next day, and we left for Wardha.

Kumudini came from an extremely orthodox family. Her husband's family were descendants of great

---

[275]J.C. Kumarappa (1892–1960) was an economist and a Gandhian.
[276]Bharatan Kumarappa (1896–1957) was a Gandhian and an author.
[277]Kumudini was the pen name of Tamil writer Ranganayaki Thatham (1905–86).
[278]A family closely associated with the shrine of Srirangam.

Vaishnavite preceptors, and even now count several North Indian royal families, in particular the House of Dharbhanga[279], among their disciples. As her husband was accorded such an exalted status, it was necessary for Kumudini to follow all traditional practices. Despite the devotion and faith she had in Gandhiji, she refused to partake of any food other than milk and *sattu*[280] flour during her three-day stay at the ashram.

Arrangements were then underway there for Vinoba Bhave to undertake individual satyagraha[281]. He was a great soul from Maharashtra. He had believed initially in attaining India's independence through force but after meeting Gandhiji became a firm believer in non-violence. He stayed at Paunar, a village around five miles from Wardha. There, he started village industries for making leather slippers and bags, the hides for which came from cows that had died of natural causes.

Vinoba Bhave could read, write and speak 14 languages. He also conducted a lot of research on non-violence as a creed. One of his preoccupations was whether a man could live on four annas a day. At that time, it was believed that the average Indian earned one-and-a-half annas, so he took up this topic.[282]

---

[279] A zamindari in Bihar.
[280] A mixture of ground pulses and cereals.
[281] Individual satyagraha was an idea of Mahatma Gandhi's wherein individuals could assert their right to freedom of expression, but not demand independence. It lasted till 1942.
[282] An anna was one sixteenth of a rupee in pre-decimal-currency days.

Kaka Kalelkar[283] was from Maharashtra and a close associate of Gandhiji. He was a great intellectual, and he began the formation of national universities on the advice of the Mahatma. He and others like him began the Gandhi Seva Sangam, which aimed to take up all the non-political aspirations of the Mahatma and fulfil them. They also began the Indian Weavers Association. Others such as Krishnadas Jaju[284] and Shankarrao Deo[285] joined these efforts.

While I was at Sevagram, I met Sushila Nayyar[286] for the first time. She had just joined the ashram. The sister of Pyarelal[287] and a child widow, following Gandhiji's advice, she qualified as a doctor. I felt really happy to have met so many patriots during my stay.

Father Goes on a Vacation

In 1941, individual satyagraha began all over the nation. Gandhiji had first permitted only Vinoba Bhave to

---

[283]Kaka Kalelkar, aka Dattatreya Balkrishna Kalelkar (1885–1981), was a Gandhian, freedom fighter, journalist and social reformer.
[284]Krishnadas Jaju (1882–1955) was a prominent social worker, a Gandhian, and secretary of the Congress.
[285]Shankarrao, aka Nanasaheb Deo (1895–1974), was a Gandhian, Secretary of the Congress, and Member of the Constituent Assembly.
[286]Sushila Nayyar (1914–2001), personal physician of Mahatma Gandhi, was a freedom activist and later health minister, Government of India.
[287]Pyarelal Nayyar (1899–1982) was personal secretary to Mahatma Gandhi after Mahadev Desai.

undertake this. Later, with his permission, other Congress members took it up one by one. Madras Congress Secretaries Kamaraj Nadar[288] and Obaidullah Sahib[289] went to prison for embarking on individual satyagraha. Many women too were incarcerated for this, including my friends Ammu Swaminadhan, Radhabai Subbaroyan, Manjubhashini and M.S. Balammal.

The year 1941 was when the nation and I experienced a great shock. As was his wont, every year, my father went on his annual vacation to Kodaikanal. As my mother and my brother's wife were both unwell, Father was accompanied by just Kasturi the cook, and the driver. A telegram came in the last week of April informing us that Father had been running a high fever for three days and that one of us, other than Mother, ought to come at once. I, therefore, left immediately, with the other cook as my escort.

When I reached Kodaikanal, Father's temperature was 103 degrees. Dr Sitapati, who was also vacationing there, was treating him. He was of the view that it was the filaria that afflicted Father periodically. We waited for three days, but when the temperature did not subside

---

[288] K. Kamaraj/Kamaraj Nadar (1903-75), active participant in the freedom struggle, member of the Congress, ardent follower of Satyamurti, and between 1954 and 1963, the chief minister of what was then Madras State and now Tamil Nadu. Remembered for putting his state on the Indian map of India and for the probity he brought into public life.

[289] V.M. Obaidullah Sahib (1905–58) was a freedom fighter and later, member of the Rajya Sabha.

and Father became delirious, I decided to move him to Madras.

I was terrified and worried. On arrival to the city, he was attended to by Dr A. Srinivasan but the fever never left him, though it subsided now and then. Father did not respond to whatever treatment was given. He sternly refused to be shifted to a nursing home or allow a nurse to care of him at home. My mother and I waited on him night and day. Dr Guruswami[290] began treating him towards the end. Neither he nor Dr Srinivasan informed us that Father was unlikely to survive.

On 19 May 1941, I was giving my father his coffee. As he was very weak, Kasturi the cook was propping him up. After a couple of sips of coffee, I noticed Father's eyeballs rolling upwards. The next minute his head slumped on the pillow.

As his younger brother Venkatesa Iyengar lived close by, he and other relatives soon assembled at our home. The funeral was over by 3.00 p.m. the same day. The obsequies lasting 13 days were completed by my brother at our residence, as per Vaishnavite traditions and in a fitting manner.

Perhaps my father had had a premonition that he would pass away soon, for, unbeknown to the rest of us family members, he had written his will the previous year. He had divided his assets equally between my mother, my

---

[290] Dr M.R. Guruswami Mudaliar (1880–1958) was a prominent physician of Madras.

brother and me. He had included a line in the document to the effect that he greatly appreciated the social service that I was doing. In the midst of all the sorrow, this sentence gave me solace. I realized that though he did not like my involvement in politics, he was happy with the social service I was doing to uplift the people. Even after his demise, it is that statement of his that till today blesses me and guides me in my service to society.

My father often said to me that he considered politics to be a dirty game, and that he did not want women to take part in it. He did not think highly of women's independence, and in matters concerning us women, he was very strict. He did not like the view that women ought to be educated, employed and earn well. But he championed the demand for their equal right to property. He felt they ought to have all rights, be respected and protected.

My Diamond Jewellery

Around six months prior to my father's demise, my son Krishnaswami resigned from the Indian Bank in Bombay on grounds of ill health and returned to Madras with his wife. His father-in-law was the then income tax officer at Karachi. He wanted his daughter and her husband to spend a couple of months with him and took them there.

On 4 July, I shifted into Meru, the house my father had built for me on Moubrays Road. I had long nursed a desire to donate my jewellery to Mahatma Gandhi for the

Gandhiji's Failure

nationalist cause. But I did not want to do this without my father's permission. In any case, I did not have absolute right over my jewellery. Out of fear of my father, I kept postponing this desire. Now he was no more. What was to be done? I had lived for 41 years under the care of my parents. Now I had to take care of my family on my own. No matter how stubborn I was, and despite my becoming involved in the freedom movement against my father's wishes, I had never thus far had the courage to take a single decision on personal matters. I had not even thought of such a possibility. But now I realized I was on my own.

Before I embarked on my new journey, I decided to fulfil my desire regarding my jewellery. I sought my mother's view. She left the decision to me. I did not probe further into her feelings. After all, I had got permission. I think it was the first week of June that I took my jewellery and left for Sevagram to meet Gandhiji. I gave them to him and he passed them on to Jamnalal Bajaj. Gandhiji then turned to me and said that as per my wishes, they would be sold and the proceeds utilized in the nationalist cause. I said that was exactly what I wanted.

Gandhiji then said that though my father's demise gave me great sorrow, it was my responsibility to take care of my son Krishnaswami and my husband. He also told me that I could come to Sevagram and spend a few days whenever I felt like it. I obtained his blessings and returned home.

I later came to know that Gandhiji had arranged for

the jewellery to be sold and the proceeds enabled a girl in the Mahila Ashram to pursue her education.

A Warning to the Whites

Around this time, the British government announced that it was considering some major concessions for India and sent Cripps[291] as an emissary. But the Congress refused to accept what was proposed by the mission. Gandhiji was angered at the way the British were refusing to understand Indian expectations. Therefore, with the permission of the Congress Executive Committee, he launched the Quit India Movement. The campaign that he undertook towards this in 1942 shook the British establishment. Many began sending their wives and children back to their motherland.

Meanwhile, the war was gathering momentum. Rumours abounded that after the fall of Singapore, India would be targeted next. The British government anticipated that should the Japanese invade India with the assistance of the INA, entire ranks of the Indian army would join them, and the people would welcome them. They also felt that Gandhiji and the Congress were eagerly awaiting the return of Subhas Babu. On the basis of this erroneous conjecture, the British government ordered the incarceration of Gandhiji, Kasturba, Mahadev Desai

---

[291] Sir Stafford Cripps (1889–1952) was a barrister, a Labour politician and a diplomat.

Gandhiji's Failure

and Mirabehn at the Aga Khan Palace in Poona. This was considered a secure location as it was close to the large army base at Kirkee. As the government now feared the power of Gandhiji, he was no longer treated as an ordinary prisoner who could be housed at the Yerawada Jail. He had to be kept in isolation. Congress leaders all over the country were arrested, and in Madras, Satyamurti, Muthuranga Mudaliar and Bhaktavatsalam too were imprisoned.

These arrests greatly angered the nation. Some of the Congress followers and disciples of Gandhiji adopted guerrilla tactics. They surreptitiously printed and distributed handbills against the government, and also damaged railways tracks and cut power and telegraph cables. They desired to disrupt the working of the government as much as possible. In Madras, members of the Hindi Prachar Sabha and others such as Sa Ganesan[292], and in the North, leaders such as Sucheta Kripalani[293] and Kalpana Datta[294] were at the forefront of these activities. As the police spread a dragnet for these people, they went underground and emerged only in disguise.

---

[292] Kamban Adipodi Sa Ganesan (1908–82) was a freedom fighter and a Tamil activist.

[293] Sucheta Mazumdar Kripalani (1908–74) was a freedom fighter, and later, the first woman to become a chief minister in India, heading Uttar Pradesh in the 1960s.

[294] Kalpana Dutta (1913–95) was a revolutionary and a communist leader.

Refugee Camps

The government constituted Air Raid Patrols (ARP) in the city owing to fear of bombardment by Japanese fighter planes. This had a women's wing which was headed by the prominent social worker Mary Clubwala Jadhav[295]. Classes were conducted at various places, especially for women in slums, on where they needed to hide during blackouts and air raids. They were also trained in first aid. Janammal and I underwent training and then conducted camps at various slums. Bomb-proof shelters and underground bunkers were built in the gardens of large bungalows and on roads so that people could hide.

As the war intensified in 1943, and Japan invaded Burma, Indians began to flee that country by foot, ship and air. At that time, I was nominated as the representative of the Women's Indian Association to the Madras Corporation's council. A special meeting of the council was called, and a resolution was passed that those returning to India needed to be welcomed and rehabilitated.

A Burma Refugee Camp was established with the help of the public at a large, rented bungalow on Spur Tank Road. In this facility established by the Corporation council, and with assistance from prominent citizens, many came to serve as volunteers. Members of the Corporation

---

[295]Mary (Mehr) Clubwala Jadhav (1909–75) was a social worker and the first woman sheriff of Madras.

council such as T.S. RamaswamiIyer[296], V. Chakkarai Chetty, and Mary Clubwala Jadhav, and volunteers, such as myself, Janammal, Manjubhashini, and others, served here. P.K. Kalpakam was of great help to me in attending to the refugees. Each morning, Janammal, Kalpakam and I would leave home after breakfast in my car. We carried with us coffee in a flask, a vessel of drinking water, snacks and a first-aid kit. We returned home only after 6 p.m.

When those who left Burma by foot reached the border town of Chittagong, arrangements were made to send them to their respective home states. Those who had to go South were sent to Calcutta for their onward journey. We received them at the railway station, and then brought them to the camp in specially designated buses. We then got details of where they needed to go and made arrangements accordingly. We often wept on hearing the heart-rending narratives of those who stayed on at the camp. Sometimes, Janammal, Kalpakam, Mary Clubwala Jadhav and I would go to the harbour to receive refugees and bring them to the camp.

Is it possible to even put down in words the tragic stories of those who had walked back to India from Burma? Husbands who had lost wives, parents separated from children, children without parents, those who'd had nothing to eat and drink other than wild plants and water from streams, those who had lost near ones to

---

[296] T.S. Ramaswami Iyer was President of the Madras Corporation in 1931/1932.

fevers, those who had returned empty-handed, having lost everything to burglars on the way...we received them all, made arrangements for their food, clothing and medical assistance. We heard their pathetic stories and offered solace. The tales we heard from them far surpassed any horror story that we had read. It was so frightening.

Our principal task was to keep these people in the camp for a few days, and then send them on to their respective native towns or villages. Some people brought bundles of Burmese currency. We had to assist in getting these converted to Indian rupees.

One poor family comprising a Brahmin priest, his wife and three small children had walked all the way from Burma to Chittagong, and then travelled by train from Calcutta to Madras Central. It had taken them two months to come from Rangoon to Madras. As soon as the train steamed into Central station, the wife and the three kids got down but not the husband. He had died minutes ago—the rigours of the journey and the starvation had finished him. Even today, I cannot forget the screams of the woman and her three children. Having performed the cremation, Janammal and I brought the rest of the family to our home. After a few days, we arranged for the woman's sister from Palghat to come and take them with her.

Members of the Gujarati community came forward to donate clothes, food packets and sweets in large numbers. There were around 30 children in the camp about whom we had no details of names, parents, or hometowns. We had to find a permanent solution for them. Dr Muthulakshmi Reddy took them under her wing at her Avvai Illam. The government agreed to help monetarily in the care of these children.

Similarly, there were around 50 orphaned young women in the camp. They had no relatives or places to stay in. The Ramakrishna Home came forward to take care of them. A house on D'Silva Road was taken on rent for this, and Rajamma, a member of our association, was made the matron. Government grants of Rs 30 per member were given to the Ramakrishna Home. They purchased their necessary provisions with this and cooked their own food. Whenever we visited them, we offered whatever solace we could. We took classes for them, taught them to read, write and sew. Gradually, the older women managed to become independent and leave the home. The younger ones were admitted to the Seva Sadan[297] and the Ramakrishna Home camp was closed.

The refugee camps functioned for four months and then, with the gradual reduction of numbers, were closed altogether.

The Bombing of Madras

In 1942, a Japanese bomb fell near Royapuram. As it is, the city was suffering from blackouts, air-raid sirens, and the fear of impending bombing. When the bomb actually

---

[297] An institution for women run by Lady Andal Venkatasubba Rao.

fell, the people were terrified. They piled their belongings on carts and fled to the villages. The government announced that those not involved in essential services could leave the city[298].

As my brother's wife was unwell, he decided to stay back. But he encouraged his children, my mother and me to leave for the outskirts. We shifted to a small house in the middle of a mango grove in the village of Thiruvoor, just outside Thiruvallur. The roads of the city were deserted. The shops and hotels closed. Vehicles did not ply, and there was an eerie silence everywhere. Lights were switched off in the evenings. Even if they were allowed to remain on, they flickered dimly as the power supply was intentionally at low voltage. On seeing even these dim lights, the ARP wardens would come over immediately and ask for the lights to be turned off. The windows had black curtains.

What can I say about the sight of cupboards and cots loaded on bullock carts, heading towards the villages? How could these large pieces of furniture fit into tiny rural homes? They were left on the doorsteps and suffered damage from the sun and rain.

This horrifying scenario lasted just two months. The fear then subsided. There were no further Japanese

---

[298] Ambujammal has mixed up two separate events. The evacuation of Madras, following government instructions, happened in 1942. The bomb fell on 11 October 1943, but as this coincided with heavy rain, floods and power failure, the public came to know of it only a few days later, and the reaction was muted.

Gandhiji's Failure

bombs. The British government stepped up security measures and the people gradually returned home.

Mahadev Desai, who had been imprisoned along with Gandhiji at the Aga Khan Palace, fell ill shortly thereafter, and passed away at the feet of his mentor[299]. He was a bar at law, came from a very wealthy family and was brilliant. He was a true disciple of Gandhiji and had been his secretary for a long time. The Mahatma never took any step without consulting him. The former often described the latter as his Boswell[300].

Gandhiji now announced that he and those interned along with him would all undertake a fast unto death unless released. The entire nation grew worried. People prayed for his welfare at temples. Many telegraphed to the Mahatma asking him to give up his fast. They also petitioned the Viceroy that Gandhiji ought to be released. Janammal, Radhabai Subbaroyan and I went to Poona to meet Gandhiji.

On our return, a meeting to caution the government over its inaction was organized at Egmore, under the leadership of Ammu Swaminadhan, Radhabai Subbaroyan and Manjubhashini. As Section 144 was then in force, the police objected to the conduct of such a meeting. When the organizers went ahead nevertheless, they were arrested and sentenced to three months in prison. Next, Dr Muthulakshmi Reddy organized a prayer meeting

---

[299] He died on 15 August 1942.
[300] A reference to James Boswell, who was lexicographer Samuel Johnson's faithful companion and biographer.

which we all attended. As it was labelled a prayer meeting, the government did not object and nobody was arrested. In reality, it was not a prayer meeting at all, and we had called it one only to sidestep the police ban.

After 21 days, Gandhiji and the government came to an agreement and he gave up the fast.[301]

In 1943, my brother, who had all along wanted to give up his legal practice and go into business, set up a life insurance company[302] along with Ramnath Goenka and Kamaraj Nadar. This later became very successful, and my brother earned a good name for himself. He also demolished the old Amjad Bagh and built a new residence for himself. The former cookhouse was renovated into a residence for my mother. In the midst of all this, my brother's wife, who had been an invalid for long, died in the Tamil month of Thai (January/February) in 1943. Their eldest daughter Vasanthi was just 18 and the rest of the children were 14, 12, 10 and 9 years of age. She was studying for her BA degree then, but following the demise of her mother, she had to shoulder all the household responsibilities. My brother sent his eldest son Srinivasan (Ramu) to The Doon School in Dehradun. The second son Bhashyam was admitted to another school in the same town. The two younger children Revati and Gopal

---

[301] This is strictly not true. The British largely ignored Mahatma Gandhi's fast of 1943 and he gave it up at the request of his followers.
[302] Known as Prithvi Insurance, it was successful, and was later merged with Life Insurance Corporation of India (LIC) on the nationalization of insurance companies in 1956.

Gandhiji's Failure

studied in a convent school in Madras.

That same year, Vasanthi was married to A.C.K. Krishnaswami, the grandson of Sir T. Desikachari[303] of Trichy. The groom was then employed with the Seshasayee Group. He later moved to Madras, and with the help of my brother, established himself in business.

Mother Kasturba, that chaste woman, passed away with her head on Gandhiji's lap on 22 February 1944. It was the festival of Sivaratri.

That year, there was incessant rain in Madras, and breaches occurred at many places. The Adyar broke its banks in the south and flooded that part of the city. In the north, the Cooum overflowed and Nungambakkam, Egmore and Mount Road went under water. There was a fear that the Chembarampakkam tank would overflow and flood Mylapore but fortunately, the rains abated. However, certain parts did remain flooded. Huts and bungalows collapsed; many people's belongings were washed away. The poor living in low-lying areas were rendered homeless. I went with the Corporation councillors and distributed relief.

Owing to my going around in the water and the mud, I was afflicted with eosinophilia and suffered much. I ran a fever every day at a certain time. The doctor opined that if I let it continue, it would soon develop into tuberculosis. I was told that the wet weather of the

---

[303] Dewan Bahadur Sir T. Desikachariar of Trichy was a lawyer and an educationist.

city was not conducive for my health, and I had to move away. My husband, son and his wife remained in the city while I rented a house in Tambaram and shifted there for two months.

I had with me one of my father's cars. Tambaram was then an enormous army base. Work was underway on a runway for aircraft, and also on a proper road to Bangalore via Poonamallee. One night, soldiers from the camp silently took away my car, drove it a considerable distance, and having crashed it against a pole, abandoned the vehicle. The police retrieved the vehicle after a considerable search. But because the culprits were soldiers, no action was taken. As there were war-time emergency measures in force, nothing further could be done. I decided I could not stay on in Tambaram and returned to Madras.

I had no cold, cough or fever while at Tambaram but back in Madras, all of these reappeared. I was treated by Dr Seshadrinathan[304].

Passion for Writing

I developed great interest in Hindi when I learnt it in 1936 and 1937, and also taught the language. I began reading novels by prominent authors in that language. I read *Durga Das*, *Shah Jahan* and *Noor Jahan*, plays in Bengali that

---

[304] Capt. N. Seshadrinathan was a bacteriologist atthe Madras Medical College.

Gandhiji's Failure

had been translated into Hindi by Dwijendralal Roy[305]. I had also read Tod's book on Rajasthan[306]. I was drawn to the histories of the Mughals and the Rajputs. I felt there was a great need to translate these historic accounts into Tamil.

Premchand was a social reformer, a believer in the Congress, and a writer of novels. Following the principles of Gandhi, he did much to improve the lives of the women who had fallen in the eyes of society. *Seva Sadan*, the novel written by him, depicts the life of a married woman who fell into disgrace due to her inability to fulfil herself, owing to poverty and marital problems. It then goes on to beautifully depict how she resurrected herself.

I was greatly impressed with this work and translated it into Tamil. Through the good offices of Harihara Sarma, this was serialized in the *Ananda Vikatan*[307]. Later, Gemini Studios[308] owner S.S. Vasan[309] made it into a

---

[305] Dwijendralal Roy (1863–1913) was a poet, playwright and musician.
[306] *Annals and Antiquities of Rajasthan* by Lt Col. James Tod (1782–1835).
[307] *Ananda Vikatan*, established in 1926 and later acquired by S.S. Vasan, is still one of the most popular Tamil periodicals. Today, the Vikatan Group of Publications brings out a clutch of magazines.
[308] Gemini Studios (1940–75) was an iconic production house and studio of Madras, owned by S.S. Vasan, the charismatic movie mogul, writer, director and media baron.
[309] S.S. Vasan (1904–69, see above). The facts as stated are not strictly correct. *Seva Sadanam*, as translated by Ambujammal, was serialized in Vasan's *Ananda Vikatan*, but then, he was only into film financing and distribution. The film was financed by Vasan but directed by K. Subrahmanyam (1904–71) at his Madras United Artistes Corporation, which then functioned on the site where Gemini Studios would come up later.

very successful film starring M.S. Subbulakshmi[310] and F.G. Natesa Iyer[311].

The *Tulsi Ramayana* is a famed work that is written in the language of the common people, so that they can read it easily. I read a commentary on it by an eminent English scholar[312] who opined that in the past, people sang verses from this work even as they went about their duties in fields, forests and towns. I feel that Valmiki's *Ramayana*[313] in Sanskrit and Kamban's[314] in Tamil are works of high literary merit but cannot be read by simple people. You need a scholar to sing them and also explain the content. Tulsidas, on the contrary, wrote in the dialect known as Khari Boli[315] and set the work to metres such as *doha*[316] and *chaupayi*[317]. Gandhiji was an admirer of the *Tulsi Ramayana* and, as per his instructions, I began working on a Tamil translation. But with my meagre knowledge of Tamil, there was no way I could set my translation in metre. I contented myself with a conversational style.

---

[310] M.S. Subbulakshmi (1916–2004) was one of the most iconic classical singers of South India.

[311] F.G. NatesaIyer (1880–1963) was a railway official, a freedom activist, a theatre personality and an impresario.

[312] Ambujammal mentions the name in the Tamil script, but this is not identifiable with any scholar of the *Tulsi Ramayana*.

[313] Celebrated as one India's oldest epics, it depicts the life of Rama in 24,000 verses.

[314] Kamban (12th/13th century), whose *Ramayana* in Tamil is a classic.

[315] The work is in a dialect known as Awadhi.

[316] A couplet.

[317] A quatrain.

The story of Rama is well known, but what sets Tulsidas's work apart are the verses that describe the virtues of good company or the society of saints. I became drawn to chanting the name of Rama often. I regret that my passion for it has dimmed with time.

Tulsidas says in his work that Rama granted salvation to one woman, Ahalya, the wife of Sage Gautama, who had been cursed to become a stone, but his name has granted salvation to thousands of women. He, therefore, established through his poem that Rama's name is even more powerful than Rama himself. I can never forget this admirable sentiment.

I could only complete the translation of Bala and Ayodhya Kandas[318] of the *Tulsi Ramayana*. When I embarked on the rest, I was faced with innumerable hurdles. P.K. Kalpakam was of great help while I worked on the translation, for she was always at hand to write down what I dictated. The great *Kamba Ramayanam* scholar P. Sri Acharya corrected the errors and was instrumental in getting the book published. Due to my friendship with him, I could meet other experts on the *Kamba Ramayanam*, such as Vaiyapuri Pillai[319] and

---

[318] The first two of the six sections of the Ramayana.

[319] S. Vaiyapuri Pillai (1891–1956) was a lawyer and a renowned Tamil scholar. He was the editor of the Tamil lexicon brought out by University of Madras in the 1920s.

TKC[320]. I also got introduced to the writer Kalki[321]. Due to these friendships, I developed a great interest in the Tamil language. But I cannot say I attained scholarship in it.

On completing the translation, I took it to Gandhiji to get him to write a foreword. He gave me a short one and then said that it was his great desire that just as I had translated the *Tulsi Ramayana* into Tamil, I needed to now embark on translating *Kamba Ramayanam* into Hindi! I said, 'Bapuji! *Kamba Ramayanam* is a work of a high literary order. To do justice to it in Hindi, I need to be a scholar in both languages. If I, with my mediocre intelligence, were to try this, the flavour of the original will be completely lost.'

P. Sri Acharya concurred with me. If only he had been a scholar in Hindi, he could have fulfilled Gandhiji's desire, and the people of North India would have a measure of Kamban's greatness.

Land for the Women's Indian Association

Readers will recall that the WIA was functioning in Royapettah on the premises rented from the Rani of Jaggampet. After a while, we got to know that we had to

---

[320] Rasikamani T.K. Chidambaranatha Mudaliar (1882–1954) was a Tamil scholar and an authority on Kamban.
[321] R. Krishnamurthy (1899–1954) was an author, a journalist, a freedom fighter and a cult figure in the Tamil literary world. He wrote under the pseudonym Kalki.

vacate as she was planning to sell the place. The eminent Tamil writer Guhapriyai[322] was living on Kalvivar Street. We shifted to a shed next to her house and resumed our activities, such as distributing milk to poor children, but as the space was small, we planned to buy our own building; Guhapriyai, Vasumathi Ramaswami, Savitri Rajan and I worked hard towards this goal. We needed at least a small plot of land for congregational singing, if nothing else. On my return from Tambaram, I sent my car for repairs and got a bill for Rs 1,000. The vehicle required frequent attention, and I decided to sell it. I got Rs 6,000 from the sale and deposited the money in the bank. I decided that this amount would be the principal for buying land for the WIA, but we found nothing to match our limited budget.

My daughter-in-law, who had studied till the SSLC, now left for Bombay to pursue higher studies. My son, who was an invalid, did not take up any other job and remained at home.

Gandhiji at the Hindi Prachar Sabha Silver Jubilee

Arrangements were made for the silver jubilee celebrations of the Hindi Prachar Sabha and Gandhiji agreed to preside. A women's volunteer corps was needed to assist during the 10 days that Gandhiji would be staying in the

---

[322] Swarnambal Subrahmanyam (1902–?) was a prolific author who wrote under the pen name Guhapriyai.

city, and to take care of various tasks during the jubilee celebrations. Around 80 women enrolled and this time, many from the aristocratic families of Mylapore came forward wholeheartedly. Many girls from Lady Sivaswami Iyer School[323] enthusiastically joined, and Mrs Apte of the Hindi Prachar Sabha trained them in physical fitness and drills. Among the many who underwent this training was P.K. Kalpakam.

Gandhiji stayed as the guest of the Hindi Prachar Sabha in T. Nagar. Women volunteers were on duty from 7.00 a.m. to 9.00 p.m. on each of the 10 days. They served food to guests and took care of the requirements of those in Gandhiji's entourage. In the evenings, they maintained discipline during the prayer meets and also circulated collection boxes. These were emptied the next morning, and the cash was counted in Gandhiji's presence. The enthusiasm with which the women fulfilled these tasks is unforgettable. Our joy in undertaking these activities during those 10 days, despite the long hours and having to often remain hungry and thirsty, was inestimable. Apart from the satisfaction we experienced from fulfilling tasks dear to Gandhiji, and the exhilaration that we were doing all this for him, we also considered it our good fortune that we were in close proximity to him and were able to see him often. This thought further encouraged us in our activities.

---

[323]Today the Lady SivaswamiIyer Girls Higher Secondary School, one of the oldest educational institutions for girls in the Mylapore area.

Gandhiji's Failure

Lakhs of people assembled each evening for the prayer meetings held on an empty plot in Boag Road[324]. We maintain strict vigil over the ladies' section and also threw a security ring around Gandhiji and his entourage. At exactly 5.30 p.m., Gandhiji would begin the 'Ram Dhun'[325]. This was the first and last time that Gandhiji conducted public prayer meets in Madras. Alas! Who would have thought that this was the last time we would see him?

Independent India

Stafford Cripps returned with a few associates[326], and after his departure, there was an agreement between the British government and the Congress, according to which the country was to be divided in two. Acceding to the desire of the Muslims who had thus far been Indian subjects, the regions comprising West Punjab, East Bengal and cities such as Lahore and Karachi were hived off as a separate country. A new nation called Pakistan was thus born.

The British gave India independence on the midnight

---

[324] In the T. Nagar area of Madras and now known as Chevalier Sivaji Ganesan Salai.
[325] A Hindi prayer to Lord Rama.
[326] This was the Cabinet Mission of 1946 comprising Cripps, Lord Pethick Lawrence and A.V. Alexander. Though it ended in failure, a subsequent agreement was reached between the Congress, the Muslim League and Lord Wavell, the Viceroy, for the formation of an interim government.

of 14 August 1947. The Union Jack at Fort St. George was lowered, and the Indian tricolour was hoisted. The next day, 15 August, the Banqueting (Rajaji) Hall was thrown open to the public. In the evening, we women conducted a meeting and a procession by way of celebration.

The British left and Mountbatten stepped down as Viceroy to be succeeded by Rajaji as Governor-General[327]. A ministry was formed in Delhi with Nehru as the head. Despite the entreaties of the Congress leaders, Gandhiji refused to take any office.

As soon as Partition took place, the whole country suffered a bloodbath. Minorities at all locations, be they Hindu or Muslim, were targeted and tormented. Riots ensued and many cruel deeds were committed. I do not need to dwell on what happened at Noakhali and Calcutta[328]. I do not need to also speak of Gandhiji's journey by foot at Noakhali to restore peace and wipe the tears of the people. History is witness to all of that.

At the annual meet of the WIA, which took place in Madras that year, I was made head of the reception committee. The event was a great success owing to the efforts of Mrs Viswanathan[329], Savitri Rajan, Sarojini Varadappan, Guhapriyai, Vasumathi Ramaswami, Radhabai Subbaroyan, Ammu Swaminadhan, and Dr

---

[327]Lord Mountbatten remained Governor-General till 1948, a year after Independence, and then Rajaji took over.
[328]Both Noakhali, a village in Bengal, and Calcutta witnessed some of the worst rioting possible in 1946 as a build-up to Partition.
[329]Wife of V. Viswanathan, ICS.

Muthulakshmi Reddy. Women leaders from various parts of India attended, and Anasuya Kale[330] was president. The conference which lasted three days was a grand event. Many resolutions concerning the rights of women in free India were proposed and passed. Among the notable delegates were Rajkumari Amrit Kaur, Leelamani Naidu[331], Kamaladevi Chattopadhyaya, Lady Rama Rau[332] and Lakshmi Menon.

In the midst of all this, I decided to raise a building for the WIA on a small plot of land next to my residence. The space belonged to my brother. I constructed a hall and adjoining it, a room and a verandah. Work began in 1946 and was completed just in time for the conference. I had decided that I would name the building after my father.

The Light Goes out

The annual festival in honour of the composer Tyagaraja was being observed in a grand manner at Tiruvaiyyaru[333]

---

[330] Anasuya Kale (*d.* 1959), from an aristocratic family of Maharashtra, was a member of the Legislature in the Central Provinces and later after Independence, a member of Parliament.

[331] Leelamani Naidu was the younger daughter of Sarojini Naidu, and an intellectual and an academician.

[332] Dhanvanti Rama Rau (1893–1987) was the wife of Sir Benegal Rama Rau, ICS, Governor of the Reserve Bank of India, and later a diplomat. She founded the Family Planning Association of India.

[333] A village near Thanjavur and where Tyagaraja lived all his life. Each year, a music festival is conducted at his burial spot.

on 30 January 1948. It was Bahula Panchami[334] on a Friday evening. The musical offerings at Tiruvaiyyaru were being broadcast, and my mother and I had tuned in from Amjad Bagh. At around 5.30 p.m., the programme was suddenly cut short for a stunning announcement. In the Indian capital of Delhi, when Gandhiji was walking towards the usual prayer meeting held outside Birla House, he had been shot at, and he had fallen to the floor uttering the words 'Hare Ram'[335]. On hearing this, my mother and I were shocked beyond belief and remained paralyzed for quite a while. Could this be true? Was it even possible? Initially, we did not believe what we had heard, but then as further bulletins began coming on the radio, we realized that this tragic news was indeed true.

Around two months earlier, Gandhiji had sent away all his disciples, one by one, from Sevagram on various assignments. He had then declared that he was going to spend some time in Delhi, and that he did not expect to return. He had often publicly declared he was willing to sacrifice his life for Hindu-Muslim unity. And almost every day at the prayer meetings at Birla House, there had been some disturbance or the other. Finally, the prayer meetings, which were held as expiation for the Noakhali killings and for Hindu-Muslim unity, took the life of Gandhiji. It was the country's greatest misfortune that it lost the father who obtained independence for it.

---

[334] The date of Tyagaraja's passing as per the Hindu almanac.
[335] Eye witnesses aver that it was 'Hey Ram'.

None of us could sleep that night. We were overcome with sorrow at the thought of not being able to see Gandhiji again. Kothainayaki and others came to call on me. We placed a portrait of Gandhiji in my drawing room and did the chanting of 'Rama Nama' morning and evening. Many left by flight for Delhi, and I too wished to go but no tickets were available. The cremation took place on the banks of the Yamuna the next evening at 5.30 p.m., with the rites being conducted as per Gandhiji's wishes.

We were asked by the government and the Tamil Nadu Congress Committee to conduct prayer meetings at Rajaji Hall from the next evening onwards. We did so with the assistance of members of the WIA and the volunteers of the Seva Dal[336]. M.S. Subbulakshmi joined us each evening for the singing of bhajans. On the sixth day, Bhaktavatsalam and Dr Subbaroyan brought the ashes of Gandhiji to Madras. This was placed at Rajaji Hall for the public to pay their last respects. On the eleventh day, the urn containing the ashes was placed in a bedecked chariot drawn by the women of the Seva Dal and taken for immersion at sea.

People turned up in large numbers to witness this, and all we could see was a sea of faces wherever we turned. People came for the condolence meeting at the Marina in immense numbers and expressed their sorrow. Notable among those who took on the responsibility of conducting the prayer sessions, the singing, the immersion of the ashes

---

[336] The grassroots wing of the Congress Party.

and the procession were my brother's younger daughter Revati, the daughter of Dr Vasudeva Rao[337] Sumana, Dr Rangappa's granddaughter Saguna, Guhapriyai's two daughters, and Judge Tiruvenkatachari's granddaughters Savitri and Janaki. They were all members of the Congress Seva Dal, and their leader was P.K. Kalpakam.

P.K. Kalpakam was the daughter of P.M. Krishna Iyer of Palghat, who worked for Sir Alladi Krishnaswami Iyer till his demise, and later ran a shop selling brass vessels from Kerala. His son Murthi was also greatly attached to me. Kalpakam learnt Hindi from me and also trained at the WIA in tailoring and embroidery. She later served the association in various ways and also worked there as a handicrafts teacher. She was not interested in politics but performed social service, seeking no personal benefit. During Gandhiji's stay at the Hindi Prachar Sabha, she was responsible for the daily collections, and each morning she would count out the money and tally the accounts, earning praise from the Mahatma himself. She now conducted the 13-day event following his demise without bothering about hunger, thirst or fatigue.

On the 13th day following Gandhiji's demise, we arranged for the customary worship at the Ladies Club building. V.D. Ramaswami, Janamma's brother Desikachari's son, was greatly helpful. We collected money from the members of the club for the event.

---

[337]Dr K. Vasudeva Rao was a distinguished specialist in tuberculosis and chest-related diseases.

Among the customary charities to be done, we gave Rs 200 to the Sarada Vidyalaya as *vidya dana* (charity for education). As *godana* (gifting of a cow), we gave Rs 200 to the Avvai Home. As *bhoodana* (gifting of land), we gave Rs 500 to the Thakkar Bapa Vidyalaya, and as *kanyadana* (conducting weddings), we gave money to Gokulam. We performed other charities by giving alms to the poor, and as for *annadana* (gifting of food), we made arrangements of Rs 500 with the Ramakrishna Home.

The rituals concluded at 11.00 a.m., and Janammal, V.D. Ramaswami and I left for the villages around the city in our car, carrying 500 sarees and dhotis purchased from the surplus collection. We gave these away to all the villagers we met on the way and returned home around 8 p.m.

A Centre of Learning as Envisaged by Gandhiji

Kothainayaki, Janammal and I pondered over what would be a fitting memorial for Gandhiji. Some people felt we could construct a centre for bhajan renditions and install a statue of the Mahatma in its midst. But he had himself often expressed disapproval at any attempt to deify him by installing his statue or portrait and offering worship to it by waving camphor or breaking coconuts. We, therefore, concluded that the most appropriate tribute would be to take up one of his favourite social uplift schemes and conduct it.

While I was at Wardha, Gandhiji had said, 'You should

not involve yourself in politics or court imprisonment, both of which are against your father's wishes. On the contrary, as soon as you return home, you must enlist his help and establish a second Mahila Ashram in Madras where women from all over India can come and study. This should be a centre where national integration and Indian culture are nurtured. Women who study there should learn handwork such as spinning yarn and also acquire proficiency in Hindi, English and their mother tongue. You should train them in such a way that they can go to any part of India and be successful.' Apart from this, he had also created an entire document on the syllabus, the food regime, and the budget for such a scheme. But on my return, owing to family circumstances, I could not make this a reality.

Now, at the end of our discussions, we realized we needed premises where we could implement Gandhiji's ideals. I decided I would utilize the building I had constructed earlier with my own funds for this purpose. I, therefore, transferred in 1948 to this structure all the activities I was undertaking on behalf of the WIA at Guhapriyai's house. We began charkha-spinning, Hindi classes and lessons for the elderly at the new premises. We also started a milk farm and basic classes for children living in slums. We gave this new organization the name Srinivasa Gandhi Nilayam, based on my father's name and that of the Mahatma, and registered it as an entity dedicated to social service.

A new committee was established to run this

organization. I was the president and treasurer, while Vasumathi Ramaswami was the secretary, and Savitri Rajan, Sarojini Varadappan, Ambu Ammal and Sita Ammal were committee members. A friend from Delhi brought a fistful of soil with some burnt petals and tulsi leaves from Gandhiji's cremation spot. I filled this in a copper pot which I buried in the compound of the Nilayam, and built a planter for growing tulsi above it. In the main room of the Nilayam, we built a small shrine in which we installed a portrait of Gandhiji's favourite deity Rama, and sang bhajans in front of it each Friday. Eventually, the branch of the WIA that functioned from here shifted to the Avvai Home in Adyar.

The Srinivasa Gandhi Nilayam, which began in a small way, grew over time and came to include a medical centre, a dining hall, a printing press to train women, and tailoring, singing, and literacy classes for the elderly. With an annual grant from the Central Social Welfare Board, we were able to expand the building. We were also able to conduct our activities through this grant, donations from well-wishers, and fundraising activities, such as the staging of plays.

I found my vision weakening and it became impossible for me to walk, read, or write by myself. In October 1949, I went for a check-up to Dr Gurupatham, an ophthalmologist who was also the health minister of Madras[338]. I was diagnosed with a cataract in my left

---

[338] He was a minister in the Rajaji Cabinet of 1937.

eye and had it surgically removed. My vision improved at once, but within three months I suffered a retinal detachment and again found it difficult to see. It was at this time that M.S. Balammal joined me. She was from the Kunniyur family and the great-granddaughter of Dr Sir S. Subramania Iyer. Her presence was of great assistance to me when I could not see well. On coming to know that in Delhi a certain Dr Agarwala was adopting new methods of treating vision problems, I went there with Balammal as my companion.

While I was being treated, the Constituent Assembly was meeting in Delhi to debate a Constitution for India. This was a very fruitful exercise, and the recognition of equal rights for women and men in it was applauded by the WIA, the Madras Women's Association and all other similar organizations.

General elections, the first of their kind in free India, were held in 1952. Campaigning was conducted with full vigour and enthusiasm, and the Congress emerged victorious. Misled by a few friends, and much against my advice, Balammal stood for the elections as an independent candidate and was defeated. That year, my mother, who had become bedridden after being afflicted with diabetes and high blood pressure, passed away in August.

In 1953, I was operated for a cataract in my other eye. With my vision now restored, I was able to resume all my activities in full. Once again, I involved myself in the Srinivasa Gandhi Nilayam.

Supported by the Andhra Maha Sabha, Bulusu

Gandhiji's Failure

Sambamurthy and others began demanding a separate state on the basis of language. A Telugu named Potti Sriramulu[339] began a fast unto death for the cause. Eventually he passed away. Rajaji was then chief minister of the Madras Province. During the protest, the Andhras demanded that Madras be made the capital of their new state. But the Tamil Nadu Congress did not agree to this, and eventually Tirupati was given to Andhra. Owing to the efforts of Ma Po Si[340], Tiruttani was handed over to Madras.

My brother Parthasarathy's eldest son Srinivasan was married to Mahisuta, daughter of K.K. Rangachari. Her mother was one of T.V. Sundaram Iyengar's daughters. The wedding was a grand event.

Durgabai, who had gone to prison following her participation in the Salt Satyagraha, had, on release, set up the Andhra Mahila Sabha. Her mother conducted Hindi classes in it, while she took the classes for the benefit of Telugu women. She continued her pursuit of education and having qualified with a BA from the Banaras Hindu University, also qualified in law. She later enrolled as a lawyer in the Supreme Court of India and practised there.

In 1954, a Central Social Welfare Board was begun in Delhi, with Durgabai Deshmukh as its chairman. This

---

[339] AmarajeeviPotti Sriramulu (1901–52) was a freedom fighter, a social activist and a champion of the Andhra cause.

[340] Ma Po Sivagnanam (1906–95) was a freedom fighter and a Tamil scholar.

was a department that functioned under the Central Government. Its prime objective was to encourage social welfare schemes all over the country and provide monetary assistance to organizations undertaking such activity throughout the country. The Central Government gave around Rs 10 crore to the Board each year. The Board had representatives from each state of India, and branch boards were established in each state as well. The Madras Board began in 1955, with Dr Muthulakshmi Reddy as its chairman. India, which was a police state under the British, had now truly become a people's state. The Central Government began welfare schemes that we could all take pride in. The Srinivasa Gandhi Nilayam applied to the Board for assistance, and was given funds for its beginners' school and weaving classes.

The Congress decided to hold its annual session in 1955 in Madras. Kamaraj was the chief minister. The maidan where the army camp was once based in Avadi, around 15 miles from the city, was the venue. Kamaraj Nadar, Ramnath Goenka, V.S. Thyagaraja Mudaliar[341], R. Venkataraman (Congress Committee Secretary)[342], Sambandam of Nelson Company[343] and N. Ramakrishna

---

[341] V.S. Thyagaraja Mudaliar was an industrialist, an agriculturist, a sugar baron, and a patron of arts and education.

[342] R. Venkataraman (1910–2009) was a freedom fighter, a close associate of Kamaraj, the father of industrialization of Tamil Nadu, later a union cabinet minister, and finally vice president and president of India.

[343] Arni Manikkam Sambanda Mudaliar (1910–1977) was the son of Manikka Mudaliar, who set up the Nelson Type Foundry.

Gandhiji's Failure

Iyer[344], all began making arrangements for the Avadi Congress. It was at this time that my brother's 22-year-old son Gopal was electrocuted while operating a radio and passed away. To overcome his sorrow, my brother shifted to a place called Bego Farms in Thirumullaivoyal near Avadi. He joined Ramnath Goenka in making arrangements for the Avadi Congress.

The Madras Pradesh Congress Committee began to debate on who could be made chairperson of the reception committee for the Avadi Congress. Wishing for a unanimous choice, Kamaraj proposed my name—my only qualification being that I was the daughter of the late S. Srinivasa Iyengar. I hesitated when he approached me for acceptance. I had no qualification or skill for conducting such a big event. I expressed these doubts to him, and also told him that I had no desire to say yes simply because of the recognition it gave me. I also expressed my views to my brother.

He advised me not to hesitate and that he, Kamaraj and Ramnath Goenka would take care of all the arrangements. With that assurance, I consented to being the chairperson. Balammal was my chauffeur and also my right hand throughout the build-up to the event.

Heavy rains came as soon as the pavilion was put up, and I feared it would collapse. The grounds were a quagmire of mud. We were nervous that the meet

---

[344] N. Ramakrishna Iyer was a freedom fighter and later a member of the Madras Legislative Assembly.

might have to be postponed. Kamaraj, V.S. Thyagaraja Mudaliar and Ramnath Goenka stayed on at Bego Farms and supervised the arrangements day and night. The venue was named Satyamurti Nagar. The entrances were modelled after a temple, a mosque and a church. As the entrance fee was reduced to one rupee, people began streaming in from outstation areas. There were around five hundred thousand people at the venue. U.N. Dhebar[345], former chief minister of Gujarat, was the president of the conference. Nehru, Morarji Desai[346], Gulzarilal Nanda[347], Indira Gandhi[348] and Shriman Narayan[349] were some of the important leaders who attended. Bakshi Ghulam[350], the premier of Kashmir State, and Marshal Tito[351] were special observers. The Congress Working Committee meeting and that of the General Committee were held in the second week of January in a fitting manner, as never witnessed before. It was at this meeting that the

---

[345]Ucharangrai Navalshankar Dhebar (1905–77) was chief minister of Saurashtra State, which later became a part of Gujarat.

[346]Morarji Desai (1896–1995) was chief minister of Bombay State, union minister under Nehru, and later, as a member of the Janata Party, prime minister of India between 1977 and 1979.

[347]Gulzarilal Nanda (1898–1998) was a freedom fighter, a union minister, and twice officiating prime minister of India.

[348]Indira Gandhi (1917–84) was the daughter of Kamala and Jawaharlal Nehru, and prime minister of India for several terms.

[349]Shriman Narayan (1912–74) was a Gandhian and former governor of Gujarat State.

[350]Bakshi Ghulam Mohammed (1907–72).

[351]Marshal Josip Broz Tito (1892–1980) was president of the Socialist Federal Republic of Yugoslavia and a close friend of Jawaharlal Nehru.

resolution to establish a socialist pattern of society was first passed.

On 4 February 1955, my husband, who had been ill with cardiac problems for a month, passed away.

Vinoba Bhave in Madras

That same year, Vinoba Bhave, having begun his Bhoodan Movement, toured Bihar and other provinces and came to Madras. A Bhoodan conference was held in Kanchipuram under his leadership. Jagannathan, head of the Tamil Nadu Bhoodan Committee, and his wife Krishnamma[352], undertook a journey by foot with Vinobaji. From Kanchipuram, they went south on foot, via Chengalpattu. O.V. Alagesan[353], I, and a few others joined them on foot for ten days. People came forward to donate land to the Bhoodan Movement so that it could be distributed among the landless. Residents of the city also donated funds generously for the digging of wells and the purchase of implements and cattle.

A camp for the Bhoodan volunteers was held at Srinivasa Gandhi Nilayam. They went from there to the neighbouring areas and obtained documents donating land and also collected money. Vinobaji constituted the

---

[352] Sankaralingam (1912–2013) and Krishnammal Jagannathan (*b.* 1926) were both freedom fighters and later tireless champions of the Bhoodan Movement.
[353] O.V. Alagesan (1911–92) was a freedom fighter, a member of the Constituent Assembly, and a member of Parliament.

lands he had obtained in Chengalpattu into a co-operative farm and got some landless people to move into it. He also made all arrangements to ensure that their lives would be comfortable there. Having conducted the Bhoodan Movement in Madras, he continued his walking tour northwards.

Chairman's Post

One afternoon in July 1957, Durgabai called me on the phone and asked me to go over to see her. I met her that evening at her residence. As Dr Muthulakshmi Reddy was ageing, she requested that I take over the post of chairman of the Madras Social Welfare Board. I considered this to be an activity in keeping with Gandhian ideals and in October 1957, formally accepted charge as chairman.

I appointed M.S. Balammal as my private secretary so that she could travel with me and also attend to numerous tasks. With funds from the Central Social Welfare Board coming in, many social welfare organizations had come up all over Madras State. It was our responsibility to receive applications from such organizations, scrutinize them at committee meetings, and forward those that we felt deserved assistance to the Centre. Members from various districts and I visited various applicants, and based on our inspection, we would forward recommendations to the Centre. We would then disburse the payments received from Delhi to the various organizations, based on their schemes.

Gandhiji's Failure

During my tenure as chairman, I had the opportunity to travel to various places from Chengalpattu to Kanyakumari, inspect several welfare organizations, move closely with people of various villages, and get an insight into their lives. I cannot forget some of the interesting experiences I had during these tours.

In Ramanathapuramzilla[354], our Board member Kamala Sivasubramaniam and her husband were actively involved in Harijan uplift, in keeping with Gandhian ideals. They had invited me for the inauguration of a women's association at a village there, and I went by jeep. As we approached the venue, I observed a group of women standing at a distance. They were making a sound with their throat without opening their mouth. I was quite taken aback and did not know what to make of this. I enquired with those about me and was informed that this was a form of welcome and known as *kulavai*.

We taught people to spin thread from hand-operated single and multi-spindle wheels. Village volunteers known as *gram sevika*s conducted adult literacy classes at various places. Around 25 branches, known as programme implementation committees (PICs), functioned under the State Welfare Board. Each PIC was headed by a woman at the village level, and she had an office and a jeep. At the zilla level, there were women heads, and each had an office and a jeep as well. These women were greatly

---

[354]An administrative area.

instrumental in ensuring that several welfare schemes were implemented in the zillas.

I had once gone to Mudukulathur, a village in Ramanathapuram Taluk. As it was less than a year since the unrest there[355], people were still recovering from the trauma. The police, on coming to know of our arrival, informed us that we could not go around on our own and had to be accompanied by an escort at all times. It was more a fetter of love. That night, Balammal and I stayed at the PIC office along with the gram sevika. At around 2 a.m., this woman shrieked, 'He has come! Oh, he has come!' and fell on Balammal. We awoke with a start and conducted a search all around. There was no one. The door too remained latched. When we asked the gram sevika why she had screamed, she said someone had flashed a torch on her face.

Next morning, the woman narrated her story. She lived all by herself in a small hut in a hamlet close to Mudukulathur. As she was alone at night, certain untoward incidents had taken place. Some miscreants would pound on her door at midnight. Others flashed torches through the window. When she screamed out for help, people from the neighbourhood rushed in to assist and the troublemakers vanished. She had been traumatized and this led to her screaming at night.

From Mudukulathur, we went to Kadaladi. There

---

[355] In 1957, the area had been subject to terrible riots between Thevars and Dalits.

Gandhiji's Failure

was not a soul to be seen during the five-mile journey. Umbrella-thorn trees formed a canopy overhead. Wherever I went on inspection, I never failed to take in the local temples and other places of interest. From Kadaladi, we went a further five miles to Valinokku Village, which was by the sea. The police jeep followed us. The sand dunes were so high that even the jeep found it tough going. This was a largely Muslim village, and a women's association functioned here for the women observing purdah. The gram sevika here ran a tailoring class for women and a crèche for the children. I was delighted to see that she ran the place completely free of religious divisions.

At another village in Ramanathapuram, the women's association functioned in a hut. The gram sevika lived and operated from a kiosk selling soda water. As there was no other place for her to stay, a door had been fixed to the kiosk to afford her some privacy.

Ramanathapuram was a water-deficient region. Water for bathing, drinking and other purposes had to be brought from a tank two miles away. This water was turbid, and trankottai seeds were put into the vessels for the colour to clear. I often wondered how this arid land was made cultivable and how, from the grain cultivated, people made money. How could women from the cities, used to all comforts, go and stay in places like this?

At the same time, it would be impossible to not appreciate the simplicity and values of the rural folk. If you went to a village, everyone, young and old, would gather to meet you. City folk are no match to them when it comes to hospitality. They will procure idli, halwa and coffee from somewhere or the other. Every now and then, they will cut open and bring fresh doub palms[356] or coconuts. If we needed to stay the night, they thought nothing of clearing out of their houses for us. But despite all this, no matter how much we explained, it was very difficult to get them to give up their age-old practices and adopt new ways.

Pushpam Natarajan was a member of our Board. She was from Madurai, where her husband had worked as a district judge. Thanks to her great efforts, a number of social welfare organizations supported by us operated in that zilla. She constructed large buildings costing over Rs 10,000 for women's welfare associations at various places such as Batlagundu, Nilakottai, Sunkuvarpatti and Silkvarpatti, and ran health centres and other facilities in these places. Madurai had an old-age home for men run with funds from the Central Social Welfare Board. It was called Rajaji Illam and was meant for destitute men above 60.

In Trichy zilla, Dr Rajan's[357] daughter Thanjamma, who passed away recently, had established several excellent social welfare institutions. One of these was the Trichy Seva Sangam. It ran a home for orphaned

---

[356]Fleshy fruit known as *nungu* in Tamil.
[357]Dr T.S.S. Rajan (1880–1953) was a doctor, a freedom fighter and a minister for Health and Religious Endowments in the Rajaji cabinet of 1937.

girls, a handicrafts centre, a printing press, and a high school for girls. A private home for the blind, funded by the Central Social Welfare Board, is run in Trichy. Looms are operated in it by the visually challenged. In another such institution, people lacking vision are taught to work with cane and also perform on musical instruments.

I had the opportunity to inspect the free medical centres run by the Ramakrishna Mission. Similarly, I also visited a leprosy centre in Sakkottai[358], Kumbakonam, managed by Mother Raphael, an elderly nun. I also had the opportunity to inspect a large social welfare centre near Thoothukudi run by a Christian priest. It had separate schools for orphan boys and girls, a crèche for infants, and a church. He also ran a home for rehabilitating fallen women. I inspected a few Muslim social welfare organizations as well.

There is no dearth of Hindu religious institutions in South India. Even in the smallest of hamlets, you can see a temple dedicated to Ganesa or the Goddess. But there are very few such institutions that establish social welfare organizations. Of late, a few monasteries have started schools.

In the southernmost zilla of Kanyakumari, several organizations were run by Smt Kanthimathi, BABT (Bachelor of Arts and Bachelor of Teaching). I inspected an institution called the Cheshire Home that was run in

---

[358] The Salesian Missionaries of Mary Immaculate (SMMI) Sacred Heart Leprosy Centre, Sakkottai.

a large bungalow in Kovalam near Madras. There was an aged British couple living there. They had once run a tea estate in Kothagiri but with advancing age, they could not manage it. They had, therefore, sold it and settled at the Cheshire Home. They remitted the small amount they received from their homeland to the institution and lived peacefully in one room. I greatly appreciated their way of life.

Chellammal from Thanjavur was a retired inspector of schools and our Board member. Due to her efforts, several backward villages in that zilla had women's associations that were run well. Pankajam Venkatachari was our Board member from Vellore, North Arcot. She was a close friend of Miss King who worked at the Christian Medical College, Vellore. Together, the two established several women's centres. They also began a ladies' club and a children's play school. Following the desire of Durgabai Deshmukh, they also began a home for young women rescued from prostitution, or who had served short sentences for petty thefts.

Chandrakanti Govindaraju was the PIC head in Coimbatore. She was the wife of an industrialist in Peelamedu. She began a few medical centres by herself and ran them very well with our assistance. Thillaiyammal, daughter of T.A. Ramalingam Chettiar[359] of Coimbatore, was a child widow, and ran a service centre for orphaned

---

[359] T.A. Ramalingam Chettiar (1881–1952) was a lawyer, a businessman and a member of Parliament.

women and also a facility where they were trained on multi-spindle charkhas.

Where Children Ate Ragi

The Central Social Welfare Board never provided full assistance to any orphanage, but it did grant funds separately for proper food, medical expenses and the purchase of new clothes. I remember a rehabilitation centre for orphans that I visited in Coimbatore. If I recall correctly, it was run by a religious establishment. The boys recited in a charming manner the *Tevaram* and *Tiruvachakam* twice a day, and also attended conventional schools. In the morning, they were given rice and sambar. I enquired as to what they had in the evening. I was taken to the kitchen and shown two large vessels, one with gruel made of ragi and the other of sambar. The matron informed me that this was what the children ate in the evening.

I was quite intrigued. As per the directives of the Central Social Welfare Board, I first inspected the kitchen, its hygiene, and the quality of food prepared at whichever orphanage I happened to visit. I saw several such organizations where they imparted education and vocational training as per the guidelines. But I would always feel sorry for the children—they had weak limbs and appeared exhausted. They were unenthusiastic in class and often fell asleep—all because of lack of proper nourishment.

At this orphanage, however, the children were markedly different. They appeared well nourished and energetic. They sang the *Tevaram* in ringing voices. I attributed all this to the ragi they ate. Just plain rotis, rice and sambar do not impart bodily strength.

Through the good offices of the Care Foundation from the USA, powdered milk is now being made available to children in orphanages and schools.

I had also cautioned some badly run private welfare institutions. Many of these were simply seen as employment opportunities for the managing family. The husband would be the founder, the wife the teacher, and the inmates the children of this couple and those of their near relatives! But I can assert that by and large, most welfare institutions are run well.

Shortly after the demise of Kasturba, a fund was collected. Gandhiji had desired that this money be utilized in appointing gram sevikas at various villages. Dr Soundaram Ramachandran[360] was greatly involved in the implementation of the Mahatma's ideals. She was the third daughter of T.V. Sundaram Iyengar. She began a gram sevika training centre at Thiruvanmiyur in Madras. Within a couple of years, she established Gandhi Gram in a large campus at Dindigul, and made arrangements

---

[360]Dr Soundaram Ramachandran (1904–84), the daughter of industrialist T.V. Sundaram Iyengar, was widowed early but chose to qualify as a doctor. A Gandhian, she and her second husband Ramachandran focused on social welfare. She served as union deputy minister for education.

for all of the Mahatma's socially progressive schemes to be implemented there. She also established the Kasturba Gram near Erode as an equivalent facility for women.

Sarojini Varadappan and Mary Clubwala Jadhav were members of the Social Welfare Board. The latter ran separate homes for boys and girls at Adyar. The former ran a women's association and a medical centre at her native place of Nazarathpet. She also funded a high school at Poonamallee that runs in her name. As she was a member of the Central Social Welfare Board, she rendered invaluable assistance to the Madras branch.

Parvati Srinivasan[361] was Dr Sitapati's daughter. Apart from running a medical centre at Velacheri, she also ran a garments unit for women. Manjubhashini was the daughter of the well-known lawyer Narasimha Iyer. Like me, she was also involved in social service. She took great pains to establish Bala Mandir, a centre for young children. Saraswathi Pandurangam[362], a veteran Congress volunteer, ran an orphanage for women in Tiruvottiyur.

Most of our PIC heads were village women who had not received much of an education, but they very successfully managed social welfare schemes. Travelling by jeep is not easy for women. But it was Durgabai, to whom the credit ought to go for bringing together women from diverse backgrounds to serve the people

---

[361] Parvati Srinivasan (1914–2000). She was secretary and an active member of the WIA till her demise.
[362] Saraswathi Pandurangam (1913–91) was a Gandhian and freedom fighter who had courted arrest.

and, therefore, the nation.

The community of women can never forget the manner in which she, during her tenure as chairman of the Central Social Welfare Board, introduced as per Nehruvian ideals several schemes for the welfare of women and children. It was also she who ferreted out the latent strength of women, hidden thus far in various nooks and crannies of the land, and harnessed it for the betterment of the nation.

Resignation and Recognition

I considered the post of chairman of the State Social Welfare Board to be one filled with serious responsibilities, and following the weakening of my eyesight, I realized I could not fulfil the requirements. I, therefore, resigned.

In 1964, the Central Government was pleased to recognize my contributions to social welfare by conferring the Padma Shri on me.

My aunt Janammal is now 85 years old. Last year, the government, in appreciation of her participating in the freedom struggle and courting imprisonment, gave her a tamrapatra[363], recognizing her as a *tyagi*. This heroine, who tirelessly supported me in every activity, is now, in her old age, living with me. Similarly, I too was honoured by the government, who gave me a tamrapatra last year.

---

[363] A copper plate, it was instituted in 1972 when India celebrated the silver jubilee of its Independence.

I would like to now write about three great people whose paths crossed mine at various times in my life, and who instilled in me the desire to be of service to the nation, practise devotion to God, and have high ideals in life.

The first was a karma yogi who I consider a divine incarnation, the second was a devotee of Murugan, and the third was a *siddha*—a realized soul.

Gandhiji—The Divine Being

Gandhiji really does not need me to write in detail on him. After all, this book is filled with his deeds and greatness. If life be an ocean, then to cross it, each person needs a worthy vessel or craft. A proper navigator is also needed. In this ocean of life, storms by way of difficult times will occur; whirlwinds too. A boat that gets caught in these will sink to the bottom. When such a situation happens, the person caught in this sea of sorrow, owing to some good deeds in previous births, gets assistance from some lighthouse. Guided by that, the person does not sink in the ocean of worldly suffering, and gradually reaches the other shore by way of good opportunities. I speak from experience.

It was in exactly such a difficult situation in my life that Gandhiji intervened. I can say that I enjoyed a rebirth because of him. He was the man who instilled in me nationalistic fervour and high ideals that gave my life a new direction.

There comes to my mind a verse in the *Ramayana* where Sage Valmiki asks Sage Narada if in the whole wide world, there exists a person who is the repository of all virtues, is brave, straightforward, truthful, unwavering in discipline, and compassionate. The answer is Lord Rama. Whenever I think of Gandhiji, I am reminded of this verse. In my mind, he assuredly had all these attributes, so he is to me the epitome of mankind and a divine incarnation.

The Murugan Devotee

When my eyesight was failing, Krithivas brought a devotee of Murugan to see me. He would continuously be chanting 'Harohara', thereby invoking the divine. He did not cut his nails, which had therefore grown long and curved. He ate only ragi. We referred to him as Nails or Harohara! He would forever be lost in meditation, and he offered love and solace to all those who came to have his darshan. I had great veneration for him, and whenever he came to Madras, he came home. When the Avadi Congress was planned, he stayed at Tirumullaivoyal and continuously showered his blessings for the event's success. This saint gave me a *vel*[364] made of silver and asked me to worship it. He then departed for Palani, where he stayed at the Sadhuswami Mutt and attained samadhi there.

---

[364] A spear, symbolic of the deity Murugan.

Siddha

I was always greatly interested in divine worship and spiritual pursuits. A friend who knew of this brought a turbaned individual to see me. I offered my respects to him, and the next minute the fragrance of sandalwood enveloped my whole house! He extended his palm towards me and it was full of sandal powder which accounted for the fragrance. That was his first divine gift to me. This was Karai Siddhar, a great soul.

Andankoil is a village near Kodavasal[365]. There, on the banks of the Kudamurutti River is a vast empty space, in the midst of which is a giant banyan tree. Under it is enshrined an ancient idol of Veera Anjaneya. The aerial roots of the tree form a shrine for this stele. There were many attempts to build a temple, but something or the other prevented these plans from materializing.

The siddha made great efforts and succeeded in building a kitchen for the preparation of divine offerings to the deity. He also built a bamboo bridge across the river to whose inauguration he invited me. I went and had darshan of Hanuman. Standing on the opposite bank, the temple and the banyan tree seemed to be on an island. This natural beauty filled my being and I returned home.

Whenever he came to Madras, he stayed at my home. His disciples included K.B.S. Mani[366], Nataraj

---

[365] A panchayat town in Tiruvarur District of Tamil Nadu.
[366] KathirvelBala Subramani was a social reformer, a politician, and a member of the Madras Legislative Assembly in the 1950s.

and Sakuntala[367]. He fell ill in 1964 and passed away at Madhukkarai. In his memory, I raised a pavilion at my residence, installed an idol of Sri Raja Rama in it, and performed bhajans once a month there.

My Life Today

I had earlier mentioned that my brother shifted to Tirumullaivoyal around the time of the Avadi Congress. There he built a temple for Vaishnavi Devi, the idol that he worshipped, and conducted the rituals in a simple manner. Over time, he built several dwellings for housing itinerant mendicants and holy men, all around the temple. To take proper care of these visitors, he created the Sanmarga Sangam, a public trust. Likewise, to ensure proper daily worship of Goddess Vaishnavi, and to celebrate the festival of nine nights, Navaratri, in a befitting manner, he established a committee whose members were named Sri Vaishnavi Sevaks, and entrusted the conduct to three trustees.

As his fervour for Devi worship increased, he became a sanyasi[368]. He divided between the Sanmarga Sangam and the Vaishnavi Temple all his worldly possessions. He now lives in a hut on the premises. As the influence of Goddess Vaishnavi spreads from the Himalayas to Kanyakumari, the influx of devotees is ever-increasing.

---

[367] A famed dancer duo.
[368] He was known as Sadhu Parthasarathy and also as Swami Anvananda.

There are special decorations and special worship offered to the Goddess each Friday.

Old Amjad Bagh has undergone changes too. All around the main house, several lovely small bungalows have come up, and the place is now called Srinivasa Iyengar Colony.

My brother's son P. Srinivasan, his wife Mahisuta and son Haricharan are involved in business in Bangalore and live there. My brother's younger son Bhashyam could not progress in business and lives alone in Madras. He has not married. My brother's elder daughter Vasanthi's husband A.C.K. Krishnaswami is no more. She lives in a hut at the Vaishnavi Temple and leads the life of a sanyasin. She is a devotee of Sankaracharya, and while leading a life of simplicity, she helps the poor in many ways.

My brother's younger daughter Revati went abroad to study ceramics and while there, married the ace photographer Harry Miller[369]. Given his expertise, he was appointed in-charge of the photography department at the *Indian Express*. They now live in Madras and have a son and a daughter.

My son Krishnaswami is now nearing 60. Given his ill health, he could not manage any regular employment. He focuses on spiritual matters. His wife Padma now lives in the Aurobindo Ashram in Pondicherry and teaches English to the children there. As my son and his wife

---

[369] Harry Miller (1923–98) was a journalist, writer, photographer and naturalist.

have no children, they have no worldly interests and devote their time to spiritual matters.

Salutation to Lord Rama

I often ponder over how in my life I had the opportunity to meet a few great souls, and in recent times, be of service to them. It is believed that when a person takes birth, he/she brings along the burden of deeds performed in previous lives. This bag opens up, and those deeds impact the new life. In fact, one of the main reasons for rebirth, and the course of life thereafter, are the sins of past births. Though we know that our sufferings are all pre-ordained and largely due to our actions, we blame others for our misfortunes. At the same time, some good things happen to us owing to the merit we have accrued in our past births. Yet, we attribute these to our smartness and intelligence and grow arrogant! We never attribute these to our deeds of merit, and even if these were aided by others, we never praise them. Such is human nature.

I shudder to think of the size of the bag of sins I must have brought along at birth. A grain of salt can curdle a whole pot of milk. At the same time, if a few drops of honey are mixed in a pot of brackish water and while drinking it, if we can taste them, then we forget the bitter taste of the water and remember only the sweetness of the honey. My mind is akin to this latter scenario. Yes, there is no doubt that I have been a very fortunate person.

Gandhiji's Failure

I was born to loving parents in a great family in this hallowed land of India. I was blessed with companions and friends such as Janammal, Balamma, Sarojini, Kalpakam and Vasumathi. I realize it is only by good fortune that I had associates like them.

Harohara Swami would often say that we should never expect life to be uniformly happy. Worldly existence is a combination of happiness and sorrow, and these will alternate just like night and day, he advised. This is after all a universal truth.

Gandhiji often expounded the principle of the *Gita* which holds that we ought to perform our duty without expecting any return, and that the merits of our actions ought to be surrendered to God.

I have, therefore, come to the conclusion that it is best to entrust to God whatever we take up, and surrender ourselves in full to Him. I, therefore, place this book at the feet of my tutelary deity, Lord Rama. May the blessings of Sitarama be vouchsafed to all of us.